DEREK MCADAM was a financial journalist in ‛
for 20 years, writing for the *Stock Exchange*
The Sun and *Sunday Express*, before moving
Scotland in 1976 where he purchased the Wes
Hotel, Tobermory, a holiday resort with its ov
hole golf course.

The *Nine-Holer Guide* brings together Mc
passion for the sport and his wealth of writing
experience in a unique guide to Scotland's nine-hole
golf courses. There is no other source of information
detailing all 162 courses with this level of expertise and
attention to detail.

McAdam has previously written a guide to the
West Highland Line, co-written a guide book to the
Isle of Mull and co-authored the bestseller, *Who Killed
Diana?* Now retired, he continues to write for both local
and national newspapers. Remaining resident in
Tobermory, he still enjoys a leisurely round on the
beautiful Tobermory Golf Course and frequently tours
Scotland playing other nine-hole courses.

www.facebook.com/nine-holeguide

The Nine-Holer Guide

Scotland's Nine-Hole Golf Courses

DEREK McADAM

Luath Press Limited
EDINBURGH

www.luath.co.uk

First published 2009
Reprinted 2010
Revised and updated edition 2013

ISBN: 978-1-908373-60-1

The author's right to be identified as author
of this book under the Copyright, Designs
and Patents Act 1988 has been asserted.

The paper used in this book is recyclable.
It is made from low chlorine pulps produced
in a low energy, low emissions manner from
renewable forests.

Printed and bound by Bell & Bain Ltd.,
Glasgow

Typeset in 9 point Sabon and Frutiger
by 3btype.com

Map by Jim Lewis

CONTENTS

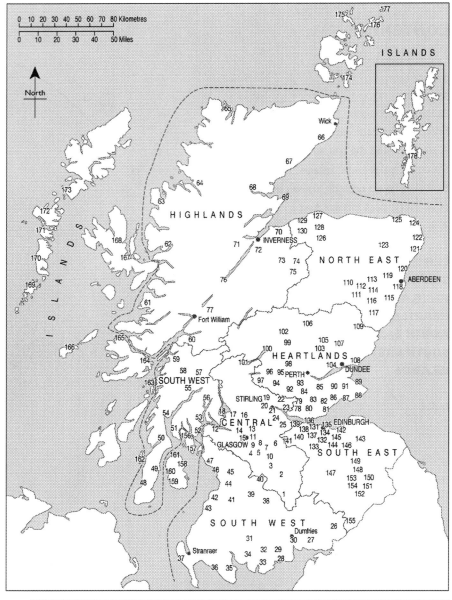

MAP KEY

Central

South West

Highland

Heartlands

North East

St Medan Golf Club

ACKNOWLEDGEMENTS

There are many people I have to thank for their help in producing this little guide. First and foremost are the club secretaries who have spent time and effort filling in my intrusive questionnaires. These over-worked and often unpaid club servants are the backbone of grass roots golf, without whom many clubs simply would not function at all. I thank them all for their devotion to the administrative side of their sport.

Then, of course, a word for Kathy, my wife, equally over-worked and underpaid, who has shown outstanding patience with my obsession for nine-hole golf courses. As a fine golfer (far better than myself) she has, at least, had the enjoyment of playing many of the fine courses featured in this book. Kathy has also taken many of the pictures featured throughout.

Thanks to Roderick Thorne of Sanday for the glorious pictures of the Arctic Skua, and to the late David Jones of Tobermory who has guided me through the intricacies of data saving and retrieval and general computer work.

A special thanks to David Howitt of Glenforsa, Isle of Mull, who can claim some 40 years experience of nine-hole golf courses, and has worn the mantle of course designer, captain and secretary – in other words a lifetime of devotion. He has willingly given me help and support in producing this guide. Hours spent reading copy, improving text and recounting golfing memories which have, in my opinion, enriched the book.

A big thankyou to Luath Press, especially Gavin MacDougall for showing faith in this project and to Leila Cruickshank, my production editor, and to Chani and Alice.

Finally acknowledgement for the many golfing web sites which have proved invaluable in the research. These include www.scottishgolfcourses.com and www.scotlands-golf-courses.com

Derek McAdam,
May 2009

Greenkeeper 'Wee' Strickland Muirkirk Golf Club

FOREWORD BY PAUL LAWRIE MBE

Open Champion – 1999

It gives me great pleasure to welcome readers to this
much needed guide book to the Beautiful Nine-Hole
Golf Courses of Scotland. These are the courses which
are so often overlooked. When planning a golfing visit
I was surprised to learn that there are 153 nine-holers
(the book now includes 178 courses) scattered the
length and breadth of Scotland, and it is my great regret
that I have played just a few of them.

It is true to say, however, that I have thoroughly
enjoyed the ones I have played, especially as my very
first golfing memories are all of nine-hole courses.
As a boy of eight or nine years old our family would
go to the nine-hole course at Kemnay, some 30 minutes
from our home in Aberdeen, and it was here that I first
began to play with serious intent.

My very first hole-in-one was at Kemnay at the
fourth, a lovely 123 yard PAR 3. I remember that tingle
of excitement as if it was yesterday.

Another nine-holer, where I became a junior member,
was at Hopeman, near Elgin. This course, which we still
play occasionally, boasts my favourite PAR 3 hole anywhere in the world. It's the lovely downhill 160 yard
fourth, with views of the sea, where the ball appears to

Paul Lawrie

hang in the air for what seems like minutes, before hopefully landing in the heart of the green. Both Kemnay and Hopeman have since been 'improved' to 18 hole courses which explains why they are not featured in this guide.

To this day we have a family membership at the Aspire Golf Centre, Deeside, where my sons, Craig 12 and Michael 8, regularly play the nine-hole course. Already they have started playing medals and show a lot of promise.

As part of my regular training I will often fire off a bucket of balls and then complete the session by playing nine holes. For me this is a perfect regime for keeping my swing in trim and practising the lessons of the driving range without the need for four hours around a full size course.

I really hope that you enjoy this guide book. Whether you are on a golfing trip with a few friends or a family holiday, the nine-hole golf courses will introduce you to many outstanding golf experiences in lovely countryside along with the opportunity to meet some of the locals who play these courses regularly.

I am happy to say that it has always been my experience that these regular players are great enthusiasts for their own courses and are usually delighted to share the secrets of their fairways and greens with visitors.

So it is with pleasure that I encourage you to explore the byways of golf and enjoy Scotland's great heritage of nine-hole courses.

Best wishes
Paul Lawrie

Comrie Golf Course

St Olaf's Golf Course. Cruden Bay

A STROLL AROUND THE COURSE

If the great championship golf courses are Scotland's greatest outdoor sporting assets then its wealth of beautiful nine-hole courses is one of the world's best-kept secrets.

Visitors arrive from every corner of the globe to play the golfing icons of St Andrews, Turnberry, Royal Troon, Muirfield, Carnoustie, Royal Dornoch, and other world class championship courses.

But do they know that there is an altogether *different* world of golf awaiting – hidden treasures in the byways, the mountains and the glens, on the islands of the west coast and in the folds of the hills and along the links of little known shores? These are the natural hiding places of our wonderful gems, the nine-hole golf courses.

They include the oldest nine-hole course in the world at Cupar Hilltarvit, the most westerly in Scotland on the Isle of Barra, the most northerly at Durness and the highest course at Leadhills (1,500ft above sea level). Sanday claims it is the smallest club in the world with less than ten regular playing members and at Scarista the unusual claim to fame is that the clubhouse is a renovated shipping container.

Castle Douglas Golf Course

It is also possible to play just nine-hole courses and still boast that you have played some of the most famous in the world. St Andrews, Gleneagles and Blairgowrie, Machrihanish and Turnberry all have nine-hole layouts awaiting your pleasure.

And it is a little known fact that some of the earliest Open Championships were played on nine-holers. From 1872 up to 1892 the Open Championship was played alternately on St Andrews, Prestwick, and Musselburgh Links, The Old Golf Course. The competition was played over 36 holes which meant playing two rounds of 18 holes at St Andrews, three rounds of 12 holes at Prestwick and four rounds of nine holes at Musselburgh Links which remains one of the most famous and oldest nine-hole courses in the world.

Our ambition with this little guide is to introduce golfers from home and abroad to the delights of the 160-plus nine-hole courses scattered across the length and breadth of Scotland. To remind them of the way golf was played in its earliest days.

Do not be misled by the commonly held belief that this is golf in miniature, an easy option and not to be compared with the demands of the 'real' game. The nine-hole courses of Scotland offer a challenge to golfers of every ability, every bit as demanding as their better known big brothers. There are many nine-hole courses where the Standard Scratch Score (SSS) is higher than the PAR, indicating a level of difficulty rarely found on 18 hole courses. These include Calderbraes, New Cumnock, Caprington, Leslie, Tarland and Musselburgh Links, The Old Course. It also helps explain why many nine-hole layouts have never been played to par – what full size course can make this claim?

They also offer a great deal more. This is golf without pressure. Very rarely will there be queues at the Starters' Hut. In fact Starters' Huts are a rarity. In a few cases there is not even a clubhouse. It is unlikely that you will be held up by slow play in front, or have other games pressing from behind. It is possible that you may have an entire course to yourself. We call it 'Millionaire Golf', but without the expense of buying your own course.

Then there is the cost. On some of these little wonders annual membership can cost less than a green fee at their famous big brothers. On one course in the far north annual membership is £10 with nothing further to pay, except maybe for competition fees. Most courses offer weekly tickets costing less that a single round on a championship links.

There is also a time advantage. Not always do all members of a party want to play golf. With a round of nine holes taking little more than an hour-and-a-half, partners will not mind wandering around enjoying the scenery, the wildlife or another local attraction. In this book we have tried to identify the flora and fauna and the outstanding scenery to brighten the interest of a non-golfing partner.

Nor have these courses been neglected by the great and good. The cream of the world's famous golfers have been known to enjoy a leisurely round on a nine-hole course, including Peter Alliss, Nick Faldo, Paul Lawrie, Ronan Rafferty, Lee Trevino and Tom Watson. Many come back year after year and some use a favourite course to warm up for a championship competition.

Just how much of a challenge do nine-hole courses offer? For serious golfers testing themselves against par the challenge is serious, for many have *never* been played to par. This does not reflect a lack of good players. It is the result of an abundance of PAR 3s and few PAR 5s. In these circumstances there is little opportunity to pick up a dropped shot. It is the very shortness of the courses that actually protects par.

All this is unlikely to worry the holiday golfer. For them we have tried to raise their interest by high-lighting the 'signature' hole on each course. The hole which best represents the very nature of the course, its terrain and demands. We have also asked for the captain's favourite hole. This is, of course, just a snap-shot in time, for the captains change but often the favourite does not. Sometimes it is the demands of the hole, but more often it is the sheer joy of playing a hole from an elevated tee, or to a narrow protected green, or the stunning view which that hole may offer.

For all of this, perhaps your interest is to enjoy a tour of Scotland with a little golf as an added extra. If this is the case then we thoroughly recommend the beautiful nine-hole golf courses of Scotland. Plan your tour around them for they will take you into every part of our glorious countryside, into wonderful scenery with mind blowing views, to meet friendly people with time to stand and chat, and to discover a world of golf that is still very much a secret.

Gairloch Golf Course
Eighth and ninth greens from ninth tee

SIGNATURE HOLES AND CAPTAINS' FAVOURITES

In our questionnaire to the nine-hole golf clubs of Scotland we asked what they considered to be the signature hole and also which was the captain's favourite hole. Their response really comes under the heading of 'casual' information, not necessary to affect the way you take on the challenge of a new course but which gives some idea of the opinions of those who play it on a regular basis – those hardy souls who can quite rightly claim to know every blade of grass on their own patch.

It is our hope that this knowledge will add a little extra to your own enjoyment of the course.

The concept of a 'signature hole' has only really come to the fore in recent years. This is the hole, it is claimed, which best encapsulates the whole ambience of the course; the terrain, the level of difficulty, the beauty of the surroundings and maybe the hopes and aspirations of the members for the rest of the course.

Captains' favourite holes on the other hand,

Polkemmet Golf Course
Teeing off at the third

represent something altogether more sinister. Scottish captains, being the hairy legged kilt wearing hard men of highland legend, almost always choose one of the hardest holes on the course as their favourite. It is clearly the challenge that gets them excited, the blind tee shot to a narrow fairway, the pitch to an elevated green hiding behind a grassy knoll, above which there might just be a lurking hoody crow, waiting to steal a wayward ball.

Wildlife

Stories often appear in the press these days of wildlife appearing in the most unexpected places – on the verges between and around motorways, in city centres and so on. Against this background it is hardly surprising that wildlife also appears on every course in Scotland. What is unexpected is the sheer variety of wildlife finding a comfortable home in the land of birdies and eagles. This is true of city courses, surrounded by housing, offices, motorways and all the other distractions of urban life and, indeed, also nine-hole layouts tucked away in the folds of remote high-land glens.

Two courses even claim to have llamas as an additional attraction, while others spotlight dolphins, porpoises, minke whales and basking sharks as occasional visiting distractions. Seabirds and the more common birds of prey are widely boasted of while others claim kites, eagles, pheasants, linnets and kestrels as regular visitors. And it is not only sea creatures and birds. There are plenty of four legged guests. Deer, horses, hares, foxes, stoats and wild goats are all there to be seen by the watchful on Scotland's beautiful nine-hole golf courses.

At the Sanday Course on Orkney they even have an Artic Skua as the Club's logo. Roderick Thorne, the Secretary, tells us that a pair of skuas nest every year on the line of the parallel first and second holes.

'This is a pretty aggressive species when eggs have been laid or are hatched', he tells us. 'In May and June players usually hold a short-iron aloft in order to avoid having the scalp whacked by a skua's feet.'

'In the summer the ground is an array of links flowers; and a variety of other isles' birds breeds on the course – ringed plover, oystercatcher, fulmar, common gull, black-headed gull, arctic, tern – occasionally even eider duck.' Roderick, it sounds lovely, even if a touch hazardous.

Similar stories come from other courses. One told us of the dangers of hooded crows. 'They soar overhead looking relaxed but slightly menacing, something like a cruise missile on holiday! It's when one of them folds its wings and dives, low and fast, you know that it has mischief on its mind. The next thing you see is it drifting back into the trees with a golf ball firmly in its beak.' On the Tobermory course

Durness Golf Course

there are local rules to cope with exactly this interruption to play – your ball can be replaced without penalty at the spot it was stolen.

Why do we mention all this when all you have in mind is to keep your head down, concentrate on the swing and make that perfect chip to the heart of the green? For the simple reason that your partner may not find your miraculous talent and obsession with stableford points quite so gripping. No one wants an unhappy companion – so the trick is to offer a pair of binoculars and a notebook and set the challenge to spot as much wildlife as possible during the thoroughly enjoyable two-hour stroll around some of the best scenery in the world.

Throughout this guide you will find pages devoted to these features, the signature holes, the captain's favourites and the wildlife. It's just those snippets of information that we hope will make your experience of Scotland's nine-hole golf courses a little more special.

Maybole Golf Course

FAMOUS PLAYERS ON LITTLE KNOWN GOLF COURSES

Not many years ago Tom Watson missed the cut at The Open and found his way from Carnoustie on the east coast to the Isle of Mull, almost as far west as you can go. At Tobermory Golf Club he quickly made friends with the members and enjoyed the course, taking several juniors around with him.

He is remembered not only for his warmth and friendship, but also for a remarkable event on the fifth. It is a short PAR 4 and the tee shot is blind with a bank rising just a few yards ahead with the fairway running along the edge of the cliff overlooking Tobermory Bay.

By any standards the tee shot was disaster – a wild slice over the bank and trees at the edge of the cliff with the ball landing on the lighthouse path, or perhaps even in Tobermory Bay.

With hardly a raised eyebrow he put another ball down and threaded a magnificent shot to the green 274 yards away. Tom studied the treacherous surface carefully from every direction and calmly putted out for his PAR 4 – an astonishing recovery executed by one of the truly great golfers of modern times! Having won five Open Championships who would argue against that.

These are the things which raise the truly great from the merely ordinary.

Tom Watson is far from being the only famous player to discover the charms and challenges of nine-hole golf.

Paul Lawrie, Open Winner at Carnoustie in 1999, has enjoyed the Inchmarlow nine-hole course as has Ronan Rafferty and many of the cast of Emmerdale. Paul has also played the course at Devenick while Ronan Rafferty has been spotted with his clubs at a number of other nine-hole courses, including Loch Ness, Scarista and Durness. The latter also claims Peter Alliss and Jimmy Tarbuck as occasional visitors. Broadcaster Terry Wogan has been seen at Rothes, the inland course some 10 miles from Elgin.

Elie Sports Clubhouse

Milnathort says they have many famous visitors, but 'they all wear masks' so we are going to respect their anonymity here.

Then there is the lovely story of the Nick Faldo 'Fiver' and the Ronan Rafferty 'Golf Ball' two competitions played for every year at Scarista on the Isle of Harris. Read all about it on p.152. Scarista is clearly blessed with some very astute members who are well aware of the marketing value of famous names on their wee gem of a course.

To spread the story that nine-hole golf courses are not merely for the lost and the lame, and to emphasise that they exist as a challenge to golfers of every standard, fame and notoriety, we have included snippets throughout the guide of the courses and their famous players.

HOW MUCH DOES IT COST?
AND A CHEAPER WAY TO PLAY

Amongst the exhaustive details of Scotland's beautiful nine-hole golf courses included in this guide there is one glaring omission. Happily this is not a mistake. We have left out all mention of green fees for a very good reason. The fact is that green fees often change from season to season and it would be a nightmare to try and keep up.

Furthermore, the cost is not the most significant detail about Scotland's nine-hole courses. It is a simple fact that our nine-hole courses offer a way to play serious golf at a seriously low cost. Few courses charge green fees of more than £15. Often it can be less than £10 and even then this will usually cover two nine-hole rounds of golf and sometimes it can be for an all-day ticket.

It comes as a complete surprise to many visitors that annual membership of nine-hole courses can often be less that the cost of a single round on a championship course. How's that for value? And this covers free golf every day of the year. As a result of the discrepancy between famous championship courses and their smaller cousins many regular visitors to Scotland pay for an annual membership at their favourite nine-holer. It takes only half-a-dozen rounds of golf to more than justify the cost of a membership, and many of these smaller courses welcome new members with open arms. There is no need for references and a reminder that the Club's traditional waiting list of 35 years has only been reduced in exceptional circumstances to 18 years for royalty and peers of the realm.

The downside of lower green fees is that the clubs have less money to spend on course maintenance. Twenty years ago this was a serious problem. Many clubs relied on the goodwill of their members to cut the fairways and greens with ancient machinery, slaving away into the twilight hours, after a hard day's

work, for little or no pay. Even then the rough was akin to a trek into the jungle.

Nowadays most courses are in excellent condition. The growing popularity of golf has meant an increase in income from green fees and membership, with the happy result that there is money for greenkeeping staff, either part-time or full time. This, together with the help of grants and low interest loans from within the golfing world (The Royal and Ancient has been prominent) and from quangos such as the Sports Council and Local Authorities, means that many courses now boast an assortment of sophisticated equipment to keep their grass and pathways under full control.

For all these reasons we do not believe that the cost of green fees is a significant factor. These days you can play on a well maintained course for very little of your hard-earned cash. What more can you ask? Interestingly enough there are ways to play your golf for even less money! Read on.

Golf Discount Schemes

Golf Discount Schemes can reduce the cost of play by up to 50 per cent and naturally have become very popular in recent years as a way of encouraging more people to play more courses. The usual formula is to pay a single fee in advance which allows you to play a

Carrbridge Golf Course

number of courses within a prescribed time for less than the cost of green fees at the individual courses.

Amongst the schemes available are Green Fee Savers, 2-Fore-1 Vouchers, GreenFree Vouchers, Golfer's Passport and the Golf Passes from Visit Scotland.

The two best schemes for the nine-hole courses of Scotland are Green Fee Savers sponsored by Bunkered magazine and VisitScotland's Golf Passes.

The Bunkered scheme offers half price golf on some 260 courses in Scotland including many of the nine-hole courses. There are 44 courses listed in the Central region, 57 in the South West, 18 in the Highlands, 54 in Heartlands, 38 in the North East and 52 in the South East. The Highlands and the South West regions include some of the golf courses in our Islands list.

All of these are listed on the Bunkered website at www.bunkered.co.uk and the vouchers can be purchased on line from less than £25 for five coupons up to around £83.50 for 20 coupons. One outstanding feature of the scheme is that part of the profits are returned to the participating clubs, which offers a compensation for less green fee income. After that all the client need do is to telephone the course of choice to arrange a tee time, and then pay half the green fee on arrival at the club. (Prices current – early 2009)

Visit Scotland's Golf Passes schemes are really comprehensive.

These are issued by all the regions featured by Visit Scotland in their brochures and on their website and, cover an extensive range of options. They are not necessarily as cheap as the Bunkered programme but can often be tailored more closely to individual needs.

To sum up: nine-hole golf in Scotland starts cheaply and, with a little forethought and planning, can be ridiculously inexpensive in our incredibly varied little country. It is generally regarded as being the home of this continually exasperating but ultimately most-satisfying of sporting challenges – from age three to 100 plus.

A FEW EXPLANATIONS

To understand the entries for each individual club a few explanations are necessary.

The length of the course: this has been shown for two rounds of the course. Although this seems to get away from the concept of nine-hole golf it has been thought necessary to make sense of the figures for par-for-the-course and standard scratch scores.

The same concept holds true for the **course records**. Course records are usually only recognised if achieved in a Club or Open competition, and in nearly every case these are held over 18 holes.

Few clubs have responded with details of course records, but there are sufficient to emphasise the relative difficulty of nine-hole courses and make comparisons with their 18 hole cousins.

What is very interesting is that a significant number of courses have never been played to par. This reflects the difficulty in picking up dropped shots on a course with a high proportion of PAR 3s and few, if any, PAR 5s.

In the Course statistics we have shown the number of PAR 3s and PAR 5s over nine holes. Course records on the other hand are calculated on 18 holes. So if a course has, say, four PAR 3s this means eight over the entirety of the round. It only needs a few of these 'short' holes to be in the region of 200 yards with bunkers, or trees, or other hazards protecting the green, and the potential for dropped shots quickly becomes apparent. If this is coupled with a relative lack of PAR 5s, where a reasonable club golfer might expect to score a birdie or two, it quickly becomes apparent why a par round can easily become a daunting prospect.

A hotelier on the west coast of Scotland once put up a £100 prize (at a time when his room rate was less than half this level) for any guest who could produce a par score in a competition. He sold the hotel 10 years later with the prize still unclaimed! It had, however, served its

purpose as a fine piece of marketing, attracting many guests to his hotel.

It is noticeable that few clubs keep a record of the best scores by lady members. There is no easy explanation for this, for there is little evidence that the clubs fail to attract the fairer sex or that they are less keen on the club competitions than their male colleagues. It would be unworthy to suggest that the best scores are not worthy of recording!

Strathendrick Golf Course

CENTRAL REGION
Glasgow, Stirling, Loch Lomond, Lanarkshire, Dunbartonshire, Falkirk and Clackmannanshire

Unlike most regions in Scotland, which tend to be easily defined, the Central Region is more amorphous, widely spread with no simple identifiable centre. It embraces the whole of Glasgow and its environs, but in fact extends from Elvanfoot deep in South Lanarkshire beside the Scottish Borders almost to the shores of Loch Tay in rural Perthshire. East to west it stretches from Falkirk close by the Firth of Forth to Greenock on the River Clyde.

Commencing our journey in the south, **1 Leadhills** lies six miles south of Abington on the B797 and is the highest course in Scotland. It is a testing, hilly course where the wind can create as many difficulties as the terrain. Watch out for the fifth, 'Oot o'sight' the signature hole, which plays across three gullies, and the captain's favourite, the first with its tight green and out-of-bounds behind and to one side.

Around 17 miles further up the M74 on the A70 heading towards Lanark at Rigside is the undulating, hilly course of **2 Douglas Water**. Well maintained and with a small clubhouse the club's unusual claim to fame is the wildlife which includes llamas as well as the more agricultural beasts of the field.

3 Broadlees Golf Course was established in 2009 on open parkland at Chapelton, a diversion from the M74, on the A726 between Strathaven and East Kilbride. As a new-build course attention has been paid to draining both the fairways and greens making this a genuine all-year-round facility. There is a modest clubhouse with changing rooms and a coffee shop and with access to a driving range and a one-hole practice hole measuring 150 yards to a full size green. The course stretches 3,039 yards with a PAR 72. The signature hole is the dog-leg, PAR 5, seventh where the challenge is a drive over a burn with fairway

1
Leadhills

Est: 1895

Tel: **01659 74456**
Leadhills, Biggar, ML12 6XT
Contact: **Harry Shaw**
Email: **stuartjlang@tiscali.co.uk**
Website: **www.leadhillsgolfclub.co.uk**
Terrain: **Moorland**

Length m **4,354**	Length l **3,872**
Par/SSS m **66/64**	Par/SSS l **68/63**
Rec m **62**	Rec l **64**
Par 3 m **3**	Par 3 l **2**
Par 5 m **0**	Par 5 l **0**

Signature Hole: Fifth, across three gullies

Captain's Hole: First, tight green with o.o.b. behind and to one side.

Clubhouse: Wooden pavilion with toilets.

Condition: Fair

Wildlife: grouse, golden plover, meadow pippets.

Location: From Leadhills village, take road at side of Hopetoun Arms Hotel on Main Street course in 300 yds.

Accommodation: Hopetoun Arms Hotel

Comments: Highest golf course in Scotland. Testing course.

Fame: Mr Panton

Caps visiting: Free

C T

C Clubhouse **B** Bar **BG** Buggy **CH** Club Hire **T** Trolley **CHR** Changing Rooms **SHW** Showers

2 Douglas Water

Est: 1921

Tel: **01555 880361**

Ayr Road, Rigside, ML11 9NP
Contact: **James Allen**
Email: **enquiries@douglaswatergolf.co.uk**
Website: **www.douglaswatergolf.co.uk**
Terrain: **Hilly, undulating**

Length m **5,902**	Length l **4,704**
Par/SSS m **72/69**	Par/SSS l **72/67**
Rec m **63**	
Par 3 m **2**	Par 3 l **2**
Par 5 m **2**	Par 5 l **2**

Times to Avoid: Saturdays April-October

Clubhouse: Small clubhouse

Condition: Good

Memorabilia: Yes

Wildlife: Llamas, deer, sheep, cows

Location: Signs to course on A70

Accommodation: Consult Tourist Info

Comments: Good challenge on uphill holes, First, Third, Fourth and Seventh.

Discount: Contact secretary

3 Broadlees

Est: 2009

Tel: **01357 300478**

Chapelton, Strathaven
Contact: **Lynn Boyd**
Email: **office@broadleesgolf.co.uk**
Website: **www.broadleesgolf.co.uk**
Terrain: **Parkland**
Length m **3,039**
Par/SSS m **72/72**
Par 3 m **2**
Par 5 m **2**

Signature Hole: 7th Long dog-leg with burns and fairway bunkers

Clubhouse: Modern with changing rooms and coffee shop

Condition: Excellent

Location: On the A726 three miles north of Strathaven and five miles south of E. Kilbride

Accommodation: Hotels and B & B's. in Strathaven and E. Kilbride

Comments: Well drained offering all-year round golf

Discounts: Available for group bookings and special offers during the winter.

C CHR PG

C B CTR D P S

Broadlees Golf Course.

bunkers at the dog-leg and then another burn to cross at the green. Good luck!

Our next port of call is the **4 Mearns Castle** Golf Academy, situated on the outskirts of leafy Newton Mearns, and a haunt for old firm players and Glasgow business men. The first hole 'Waterfoot Ridge' can be a challenge as there is a burn some 200 yards off the yellow tee. The approach shot is a slight dog-leg to the right with added pressure from tall trees to either side of the fairways and a sloping green. All greens meet USGA spec. providing all year round golf. Facilities include a 40 bay Driving Range and a teaching academy, a short game area and practise putting greens. **Bring your copy of *Nine-Holer Guide* to reception when booking a tee time and play for only £5!** That's what we call enlightened management.

Eight and a half short miles north of Strathaven Playsport Golf has established **5 The Heritage Links**, a quite elaborate new course at their East Kilbride centre where a number of famous holes from Championship courses have been re-created. This is a PAR 32 test with rolling hills, undulating fairways, large greens and an astonishing 51 bunkers to test every aspect of the game. The opening hole is a slight dog-leg PAR 4 played into the prevailing wind with fairway bunkers offering a challenge off the tee, and the course finishes with a tricky PAR 3 with the tee shot played over a tree to a green surrounded by eight deep faced bunkers. Perhaps the most interesting hole is the Signature 8th a copy of the 17th at the Old Course, St Andrews.

The next course on this journey is some ten miles east to the Dalziel course attached to the **6 Dalziel** Park Hotel complex in the centre of Motherwell and well signposted from the City centre. Dalziel has undergone a number of transitions in its history having gone from a 9 hole course to an 18 holer and then, under new management, back to a nine-holer in 2011, and is all the better for it. Set in a rolling landscape there are many hazards around the greens. The fairways

4 Mearns Castle

Est: 2003
Tel: **0141 644 8200**
Waterfoot Road, Newton Mearns, Glasgow, G77 5RR
Contact: **Russell Gray**
Email: **russell@mcgolfacademy.co.uk**
Website: **www.mcgolfacademy.co.uk**
Terrain: **Parkland**
Length m **5,084**
Par/SSS m **66/64**
Par 3 m **4**
Par 5 m **1**
Signature Hole: First, Waterfoot Ridge with a tricky tee shot.
Course Record: 59
Clubhouse: Modern clubhouse with outstanding facilities including a café, ladies gym and a massage room.
Condition: Excellent
Location: On Waterfoot Road, Newton Mearns
Accommodation: Wide choice in Newton Mearns
Comments: USGA spec green offering all-year round golf
Discounts: £5 green fee for anyone bringing a copy of the *Nine-Holer Guide*

C B CHR SHW CTR PG D P S

5
Heritage Links

Est: 2009

Tel: **01355 575 980**

Stewartfield Way, East Kilbride, G74 4GT
Contact: **Colin McEwan**
Email: **colinmcewan@ymail.com**
Website: **www.playsportgolf.com**
Terrain: **Inland links**
Length m **4,614**
Par/SSS m **64/64**
Par 3 m **4**
Par 5 m **1**
Signature Hole: 8th

Clubhouse: Golf Café adjacent to the reception
serves hot drinks, soup, sandwiches and hot
filled rolls, and there is a welcome at the
licensed Fives sports bar.

Condition: Except in unusually wet weather
the course is always in a dry condition with
full USGA spec. tees and greens ensuring
year round play.

Location: On Stewartfield Way.

Discounts: Discounts available on weekdays
between 12 noon to 4 pm.

6
Dalziel Park

Est: 2011 (restored to a 9 holer)

Tel: **01698 862 862**

100 Hagen Drive, Motherwell, ML1 5RZ
Contact: **Linda Smith**
Email: **golf@dalzielpark.co.uk**
Website: **www.lisini.co.uk**
Terrain: **Parkland**
Length **3,300 yards**
Par/SSS **72/72**
Par 5 m **1**
Clubhouse: Full use of hotel facilities, bar and
restaurant.

Condition: Excellent.

Location: Signposted from centre of
Motherwell.

Discounts: Negotiable

C B CTR P S	C B CHR SHW CTR PG

are tight with some lovely PAR 3s and a difficult PAR 5 dog leg as a closing hole.

7 Strathclyde Park (junction five on the M74) is set amongst mature woods and parklands adjoining Strathclyde Country Park, with Hamilton Racecourse on one side and a nature reserve on the other.

Also in the Lanarkshire area to the south of Glasgow is **8 Calderbraes** at Uddingston close to the Zoo Park. Test yourself on this difficult hilly woodlands course with out-of-bounds everywhere you look. The fourth is the signature hole with a long second shot to an elevated green with o.o.b. to left and right.

Situated just off the main Glasgow to Hamilton road some 750 metres from Cambuslang Station the **9 Cambuslang** course is a lengthy parkland test with a demanding PAR 5 opening hole. Unusually for a nine-holer this course has only two PAR 3s. Visitors can play only if accompanied by a member.

Closer now to Glasgow is the open parkland course of **10 Larkhall**, situated on the B7019 to the east of the town. There are few hazards to bother you here and there is the attraction of refreshments in the bar after your game.

In the extended area around Greater Glasgow and its environs there are four lovely nine-hole courses to tempt you from the attractions of this surprisingly beautiful city. Two miles east of the city centre at

7
Strathclyde Park

Est: Unknown

Tel: **01698 429350**

Mote Hill, Hamilton, Lanarkshire, ML3 6BY
Contact: **The Secretary**
Website: **www.slleisureandculture.co.uk**
Terrain: **Parkland**
Length m **6,102**
Par/SSS m **72/70**
Par 3 m **2**
Par 5 m **2**
Signature Hole: Unknown
Captain's Hole: Unknown
Location: Exit junction five (Hamilton) from M74

B CHR SHW PG D P S

Strathclyde Park Golf Course

C Clubhouse **B** Bar **BG** Buggy **CH** Club Hire **T** Trolley **CHR** Changing Rooms **SHW** Showers

8
Calderbraes

Est: Unknown

Tel: **01698 813425**

57 Roundknowe Road, Uddingston, Glasgow, G71 7TS

Contact: **The Secretary**

Email: **calderbraesgolfclub@tiscali.co.uk**

Website: **www.calderbraesgolfclub.com**

Terrain: **Hilly woodland, inland**

Length m **5,186**

Par/SSS m **66/67**

Par 3 m **3**

Par 5 m **0**

Signature Hole: Fourth, elevated green with o.o.b. to left and right

Location: Beginning of M74, east of Glasgow, close to Glasgow Zoo

C B CHR SHW CTR

9
Cambuslang

Est: 1892

Tel: **0141 6413130**

30 Westbourne Drive, Cambuslang, Glasgow, G72 7NA

Contact: **R. M. Dunlop**

Email: **secretary@cambuslanggolf.co.uk**

Website: **www.cambuslanggolf.co.uk**

Terrain: **Wooded Parkland**

Length m **5,942**	Length l **5,428**
Par/SSS m **70/69**	Par/SSS l **72/72**
Rec m **61**	Rec l **66**
Par 3 m **2**	Par 3 l **1**
Par 5 m **1**	Par 5 l **2**

Signature Hole: Sixth, dog-leg round Do'cote

Captain's Hole: 19th

Times to Avoid: No visitors except with members

Clubhouse: Yes

Condition: Good

Location: In Cambuslang

C B CHR SHW CTR PG

10
Larkhall

Est: Unknown

Tel: **01698 881113**

Burnhead Road, Larkhall, Glasgow, ML9 3AB

Contact: **The Secretary**

Website: **www.slleisureandculture.co.uk**

Terrain: **Open parkland**

Length m **6,280**

Par/SSS m **70/70**

Par 3 m **2**

Par 5 m **1**

Location: Eastside of Larkhall on B7019

C B CHR SHW

Larkhall Golf Course.
First Tee

Dennistoun is **11 Alexandra Park**, a hilly, parkland course with attractive mature trees and some tricky PAR 3s. Watch out for the seventh, the signature hole, with its ranging views of the surrounding parkland where wild deer can occasionally be seen.

Remaining south of the Clyde the journey moves along the M8 motorway and past Glasgow Airport and continues to Greenock on the Clyde Estuary where the **12 Greenock** Golf Club offers a lovely James Braid designed nine-holer as well as the 18 hole course. Enjoying spectacular views over the Clyde Estuary and to the Argyll hills beyond this is a beautifully maintained course with all the facilities of a major club, where Harry Vardon, Roberto de Vicenzo and Sam Torrance have all exhibited their skills.

Travelling north of the great river Clyde we head for Maryhill and Possil Park a relatively economically depressed part of Glasgow. Against this background the new **13 Ruchill** course is a breath of fresh air. Designed with help from celebrated Scottish golfer Colin Montgomerie this is a short but impressive lay-out and has already received many compliments since it was opened in 2009. In recognition of his help the first hole is named Monty's Mound.

Five miles north-west of Glasgow is the **14 Bearsden** Golf Course, which although a nine-hole course plays to 16 greens with 11 teeing areas. There is a putting green and practice ground and full catering facilities.

11 Alexandra Park

Est: Unknown

Tel: **0141 7700519**

Alexandra Park, Sannox Gardens, Dennistoun, Glasgow, G31 8SE
Contact: **Lynn Colvin**
Website: **www.csglasgow.org**
Terrain: **Wooded parkland, hilly**

Length m **4,016 yds**	Length l **4,016**
Par/SSS m **60/61**	Par/SSS l **64/64**
Par 3m **6**	Par 3 l **4**

Signature Hole: Seventh, PAR 3 Situated on the top of the hill, overlooking the M8 motorway

Clubhouse: Area for functions

Condition: Drains quickly

Wildlife: Wild deer

Location: At the rear of Alexandra Park

Accommodation: Merchant Lodge, Virginia Street, Thistle Hotel, Cambridge Street

Lost ball: 5

Comments: A challenge for casual and serious golfers

Discount: Spree

Clubs visiting: Contact Secretary

C P

Bearsden Golf Course

12
Greenock

Est: 1890

Tel: **01475 720793**

Forsyth Street, Greenock, PA16 8RE
Contact: **The Secretary**
Email: **secretary@greenockgolfclub.co.uk**
Website: **www.greenockgolfclub.co.uk**
Terrain: **Inland**
Length m **4,320**
Par/SSS m **64/64**

13
Ruchill

Est: 2009

Tel: **0141 276 0556**

Brassey St Ruchill, Maryhill, Glasgow, G20 9HP
Contact: **David Kerr**
Email: **info@glasgowlife.org**
Terrain: **Parkland**
Length **3,378**
Par/SSS **58/58**
Par 3 **7**
Par 5 **0**
Condition: Good
Location: Off the A81, Maryhill Road, north of Possil Park.

PG

14
Bearsden

Est: 1891

Tel: **0141 5865300**

Thorn Road, Bearsden, Glasgow, G61 4BP
Contact: **The Secretary**
Email: **secretary@bearsdengolfclub .com**
Website: **www.bearsdengolfclub.com**
Terrain: **Heathland and links**
Length m **6,014**
Par/SSS m **68/69**
Par 3 m **2**
Location: Turn left at Bearsden Cross from Glasgow.

C B CHR SHW CTR PG P S

Tillicoultry Golf Course

Off the Great Western Road lies **15 Knightswood** Golf Course with open fairways and parkland views. It boasts a difficult opening hole, PAR 4 with out-of-bounds to the right. A heavily bunkered green sloping away at the back demands an accurate approach shot.

Heading north on the A809 or the A81 from Glasgow, is **16 Strathendrick** at Drymen by Loch Lomond. Designed by Willie Fernie this undulating parkland course looks down on the River Endrick. Approaching from Glasgow or Balloch cross the bridge over the river and in 200 yards turn right into the lane to the course.

Heading west from Strathendrick on the A811 our next course is **17 Ross Priory** situated in over 200 acres of parkland on the south east shore of Loch Lomond. Ross Priory is the Recreation and Conference Centre of the University of Strathclyde and could not have a more romantic and dramatic setting. The course is open to current and retired members of staff and graduates of the University.

On the far side of Loch Lomond is the deluxe Cameron House Hotel, home of the **18 Wee Demon** nine-hole course. This is a cleverly designed and challenging course, even for low handicap players, with two holes surrounded by water, some long and tricky PAR 3s and a splendid first PAR 5.

15
Knightswood

Est: Unknown

Tel: **0141 9596358**

Lincoln Avenue, Glasgow, G13 3DN
Contact: **The Secretary**
Website: **www.csglasgow.org**
Terrain: **Parkland**
Length m **5,584**
Par/SSS m **68/67**
Par 3 m **3**
Par 5 m **1**

Location: West along Great Western Road to Lincoln Avenue

C CHR PG

Wee Demon Golf Course

16
Strathendrick

Est: Unknown

Tel: 01360 660695

Glasgow Road, Drymen, Glasgow, G63 0BY
Contact: **The Secretary**
Website: **www.strathendrickgolfclub.co.uk**
Terrain: **Undulating parkland**
Length m **4,982**
Par/SSS m **66/64**
Par 3 m **4**
Par 5 m **1**

`C CHR SHW CTR PG`

17
Ross Priory

Est: c.1970

Tel: 01389 830 398

Loch Lomond, Nr. Gartocharn, Glasgow G 53
Contact: **David Upton**
Email: **rosspriory.club@strath.ac.uk**
Website: **www.strath.ac.uk/rosspriory**
Terrain: **Parkland**

`C B CHR SHW CTR PG`

18
Wee Demon

Est: Unknown

Tel: 01389 755565

De Vere Cameron House Resort, Loch Lomond,
Luss, Argyll,
Contact: **The Secretary**
Email: **thecarrick@cameronhouse.co.uk**
Website: **www.cameronhouse.co.uk**
Terrain: **Parkland**
Length m **4,800**
Par/SSS m **64/64**

Mearns Castle Golf Course
2nd Green.

East from here in Stirlingshire there are four attractive nine-holers waiting to tempt you; Bridge of Allan, Airthrey, Brucefields and Alva. Designed by Old Tom Morris the opening hole at **19 Bridge of Allan** Golf Course is generally recognised as one of the most difficult in the world of nine-hole golf. A 223 yard PAR 3 it requires an uphill drive over a six foot high dyke to an elevated green. This is a particularly picturesque course with lovely views of Stirling Castle, the Wallace Monument, Perthshire hills and west to Ben Lomond and the Arrochar Alps.

20 Airthrey Golf Course is attached to the University of Stirling. This challenging parkland course, only a short hike from Stirling centre, is overlooked by Airthrey Castle and has glorious views of the Ochil Hills and Airthrey Loch. It is the signature seventh on the banks of the loch which provides the most demanding challenge with a tee shot to a smallish green built in the hillside and protected by water and trees.

To the other side of Stirling on the A91, in the Bannockburn area, another challenging battle awaits at **21 Brucefields**. This Family Golf Centre offers catering, a pro shop and unusually for nine-hole courses, a driving range.

Seven miles away on the A91 Stirling to St Andrews road lies the **22 Alva** Golf Club, at the foot of the Ochil Hills in the 'wee county' of Clackmannanshire.

19
Bridge of Allan

Est: 1895

Tel: **01786 832332**

Sunnylaw, Bridge of Allan, Stirlingshire, FK9 4LY
Contact: **The Secretary**
Email: **secretary@bofagc.com**
Website: **www.bofagc.com**
Terrain: **Parkland with steep hills**

Length m **5,120**	Length l **4,534**
Par/SSS m **66/66**	Par/SSS l **66/68**
Par 3 m **3**	Par 3 l **3**
Par 5 m **0**	Par 5 l **0**

Signature Hole: First, 223yd PAR 3. Uphill tee shot over a six foot high dyke to an elevated green

Times to Avoid: During competitions

Condition: Excellent

Location: East of A9 at Bridge of Allan, midway between Stirling and Dunblane

Fame: Heather Stirling (member) member of Curtis Cup Team, now turned professional

Discount: Yes

Clubs visiting: Contact Secretary

Caps visiting: Contact Secretary

C

Airthrey Castle Golf Course

20 Airthrey

Est: Unknown

Tel: 01786 466915

Airthrey Castle, University of Stirling, Stirling, FK9 4LA
Contact: **The Secretary**
Email: **sports.development@stir.ac.uk**
Website: **www.stir.ac.uk**
Terrain: **Parkland**
Length m **2,008**
Par/SSS m **54/54**
Par 3 m **9**

CH PG

21 Brucefields

Est: Unknown

Tel: 01786 818184

Pirnhall Road, Bannockburn, Stirling, FK7 8EH
Contact: **The Secretary**
Email: **info@brucefields.co.uk**
Website: **www.brucefields.co.uk**
Terrain: **Parkland**
Length m **5,026**
Par/SSS m **68/65**
Par 3 m **9**
Par 5 m **0**

Signature Hole: PAR 3 sixth, can require anything from a wedge to a seven iron

Location: Junction nine on M9/M80 to Stirling take A91 then 500 yards on left

C B BG CH T CHR SHW CTR PG D P S

22 Alva

Est: 1901

Tel: 01259 760431

Beauclere Street, Alva, Nr Stirling, FK12 5LD
Contact: **The Secretary**
Email: **enquiries@alvagolfclub.co.uk**
Website: **www.alvagolfclub.co.uk**
Terrain: **Parkland**
Length m **4,846**
Par/SSS m **66/64**
Par 3 m **3**

Location: A91 Stirling to St Andrews. 30 miles north east of Glasgow.

C B CTR

Alva Golf Course

The Alva course was established over a century ago and with its small greens continues to offer a stern test. It was the home course for Frank C. Rennie, professional at the mighty Prestwick Golf Course.

Less than three miles to the west of Alva is the **23 Tillicoultry** Golf Club another lovely course with spectacular views of Ochils. Early in the 19th century Queen Victoria thought the wooded green valley of Tillicoultry reminded her of Italy and Swizerland. This is a well maintained course and the relatively short two PAR 3s demand respect and a accuracy from the tee.

Driving south from Alva to the Falkirk area lie the last two courses in the Central Region, Bonnybridge and Polmont. **24 Bonnybridge** is situated on Larbert Road, on the A802 three miles west of Falkirk. With a yardage of 6,058 and a sss of 70 the course is longer and possibly more demanding than the average nine-holer.

25 Polmont lies to the other side of Falkirk in the village of Maddiston on the B805 to where it moved some 30 years ago. Like Bonnybridge this is another course over 6,000 yards long, with a par of 72 and sss of 70. The sixth is the signature hole, a dog-leg to a small green protected by bunkers, o.o.b. to the right and trees to the left. An equal challenge is the captain's favourite hole, the fourth, with trees on both sides of the fairway to a well bunkered small green. Watch out for deer, badgers and buzzards. In recent years extra holes have been laid out which creates the impression of playing an 18 holer.

23
Tillicoultry

Est: 1899
Tel: **01259 750 124**
Alva Road, Tillicoultry, FK13 6BL
Contact: **Margaret Kenny**
Email: **tillygolf@btconnect.com**
Website: **www.tillygc.co.uk**
Terrain: **Parkland**
Length **4,775 yards**
Par/SSS **70/70**
Par 3 **2**
Par 5 **0**
Clubhouse: Friendly clubhouse offering refreshments and a
Condition: Well maintained
Location: On Alva Road
Accommodation: Harvieston Inn
Comments: A gem of a nine-holer
Discounts: Negotiable for group booking

C B CTR

Polmont Golf Course

24
Bonnybridge

Est: Unknown

Tel: **01324 812323**

Larbert Road, Bonnybridge, Falkirk, FK4 1NY
Contact: **The Secretary**
Email: **bgc1@hotmail.co.uk**
Website: **www.scottish.heartlands.org**
Terrain: **Parkland**
Length m **6,058**
Par/SSS m **72/70**
Par 3 m **2**
Par 5 m **2**

Location: One mile north-east of Bonnybridge off A883.

B CHR SHW CTR PG P S

25
Polmont

Est: 1902

Tel: **01324 711277**

Manuelrigg, Maddiston, Falkirk, FK2 0LS
Contact: **John Ingram**
Email: **polmontgolfclub@btconnect.com**
Terrain: **Parkland, hilly**

Length m **6,092**	Length l **5,226**
Par/SSS m **72/70**	Par/SSS l **70/70**
Rec m **69**	
Par 3 m **2**	Par 3 l **2**
Par 5 m **2**	Par 5 l **2**

Signature Hole: Sixth, dog-leg to small green protected by bunkers, o.o.b. to the right and trees to the left.

Captain's Hole: Fourth, PAR 4 with trees on both sides of fairway to a small green protected by bunkers on r.h.s. and rear.

Times to Avoid: Saturdays and some Wednesdays.

Clubhouse: Large clubhouse with full bar facilities, snacks and meals by arrangement

Condition: Very good from April on

Memorabilia: Ball markers

Wildlife: Hares, foxes, hawks, small roe deer.

Location: Past Central Region Fire Headquarters. From Falkirk take first right.

Accommodation: Inchyra Grange Hotel, Grangemouth.

Lost ball: 3

Comments: Challenging course, tight fairways, small greens, great views of River Forth and hills beyond and the Forth bridges.

Discount: Bunkered

Clubs visiting: Contact Secretary

Caps visiting: Free

C B CHR P

Bonnybridge Golf Course

SOUTH WEST
Dumfries and Galloway, Ayrshire and Argyll

The glorious South West area of Scotland stretches all the way from the borders at Gretna to Oban, the gateway to the Isles, in the north. Famed for Rabbie Burns, run-away weddings, the Highroad to Loch Lomond and countless beautiful sea lochs, the area is also a playground of great nine-hole golf courses.

There are 30 courses in all, offering the possibility of a grand golfing tour through the beautiful western counties of Scotland.

From Gretna, going north on the M74, there are 12 courses in and around Dumfries and Galloway, including just one to the east of the trunk road. This is the parkland course at **26 Langholm** situated on the A7 Carlisle to Edinburgh route. Established in 1892 the course enjoys views of the rolling border hills. An unusual claim to fame is that the first captain, Thomas Moses was a director of cloth makers Reid and Taylor, manufacturers of the cloth used for Augusta's 'Green Jackets'. Give it a try and see if you can win your very own 'Green Jacket', maybe talk yourself into it having a drink at the '19th', or the 10th as we nine-hole aficionados call it. Sitting above the town the course is in great condition with lovingly sculpted tees.

All the other courses in this area lie to the west of the A74 and the next course on our tour would have been Gretna – but please do not waste your time as sadly it no longer exists. It was a fine course but it seems to have gone the way of all good things.

Not far away is **27 Hoddom Castle** two and a half miles off the A74 (M) from Junction 19 where the pleasant sheltered course is set in beautiful surroundings by the River Annan in the 10,000 acre grounds of a 16th century border keep. The captain's favourite hole is the first a short PAR 4 with a large oak tree in the middle of the fairway and a second shot to an elevated green.

A few miles east is **28 Craigieknowes**, Kippford,

26
Langholm

Est: 1892

Tel: **0772 4875151**

Whitahall, Langholm, Dumfries-shire, DG13 0JR
Contact: **The Secretary**
Email: **adizoe@btinternet.com**
Website:
 www.langholmgolfclub.intheteam.com
Terrain: **Parkland**
Length m **6,180**
Par/SSS m **70/69**
Par 3 m **4**   Par 5 m **2**
Location: Turn off A7 in Langholm Market
 Square and follow signs.

C B CHR SHW P

27
Hoddom Castle

Est: 1973

Tel: **01576 300251**

Hoddom Castle Caravan Park, Hoddom,
Lockerbie, DG11 1AS
Contact: **Kath Condron**
Email: **hoddomcastle@aol.com**
Website: **www.hoddomcastle.co.uk**
Terrain: **Parkland, beside River Annan**

Length m **4,640**	Length l **4,640**
Par/SSS m **68/68**	Par/SSS l **68/68**
Par 3 m **2**	Par 3 l **2**
Par 5 m **0**	Par 5 l **0**

Signature Hole: Fifth, dog-leg left to a green
guarded by trees. River Annan forms
boundary to fairway and green.

Captain's Hole: First, short PAR 4 with large oak
tree in the middle of the fairway to an
elevated green

Times to Avoid: Bank holidays

Clubhouse: None, Caravan site bar and
restaurant adjacent

Condition: Good with mature fairways

Memorabilia: Ball markers

Wildlife: Wildfowl, numerous birds, otters

Location: Take Junction 19 from M74 and
follow signs to Hoddom Castle Caravan Park

Accommodation: Caravan Park, Ravenhill
Hotel, Lockerbie

Lost ball: 1

Comments: A pleasant sheltered course in
beautiful surroundings

Clubs visiting: Ten per cent discount for groups

B

28
Craigieknowes

Est: 1994

Tel: **01556 620244**

Barnbarroch Farm, Kippford, Dalbeattie,
DG5 4QS
Contact: **Kathleen Roan**
Email: **kathleenroan@supanet.com**
Terrain: **Parkland with rocky outcrops**

Length m **2,782**	Length l **2,782**
Par/SSS m 54/54	Par/SSS l **54/54**
Rec m **27** (9 holes)	
Par 3 m **9**	Par 3 l **9**
Par 5 m **0**	Par 5 l **0**

Signature Hole: Third, well protected by rocky
outcrops

Clubhouse: Licensed tea room with changing
rooms

Condition: Good

Memorabilia: Golf balls and some clothing
available to order

Wildlife: Pheasants, deer, kestrels, rabbits

Location: Take A710 from Dalbeattie for about
three miles turn right. At Kippford Junction,
course on right.

Accommodation: Anchor Hotel, Kippford

Lost ball: 5

Comments: Quiet and ideal for all grades of
golfers. Good for families.

Clubs visiting: Contact Secretary

C CH T CHR CTR PG

Tobermory Golf Course

around three miles south of Dalbeattie on the A710, described by the secretary as 'quiet and ideal for all grades of golfers. Good for families'. If the family is not riveted by golf they can watch for pheasants, deer, kestrels and rabbits. For golfers the signature hole is the third where the green is well protected by rocky outcrops.

Another local parkland course is **29 Dalbeattie** which offers a friendly and relaxed welcome to golfers of all abilities and enjoys lovely views. Watch out for the 'signature' eighth, a PAR 3 measuring 156 yards, played from an elevated tee to a small green through an avenue of birch trees and guarded by a deep-faced bunker on the right. The wind can make club selection a problem and can range from a mid iron to a five wood.

North from Dalbeattie, a mile from the attractive county town of Dumfries, is the challenging, parkland **30 Crichton** Golf Course. The elevated first few holes offer good views of Dumfries and the River Nith. See how you cope with the challenging long PAR 3 fifth, the signature hole, where the green is guarded by huge trees and bunkers. The captain favours the PAR 4 seventh where the tree-lined fairway narrows over the last 150 yards.

In the famous Galloway Hills is the 'hidden gem' of the **31 New Galloway** Golf Course (take the A75 and then the A712 from Dumfries). This moorland course is a good test on super greens where the captain suggests the PAR 4 third is one to watch out for. It needs an especially good drive over a wall at 170 yards. The 'signature' eighth is played from an elevated tee and then uphill to the green over a gully and rock outcrops.

Further south in the area around Castle Douglas there are three nine-holers to capture out attention. The **32 Castle Douglas** course is on Abercrombie Road and just 400 yards from the town centre. Although a parkland course it has one steep hill where the views of the Galloway Hills more than

29 Dalbeattie

Est: 1894

Tel: **01556 611421**

Maxwell Park, Dalbeattie, DG5 4LR
Contact: **Bryan Moor**
Email: **jbhenderson45@gmail.com**
Website: **www.dalbeattiegc.co.uk**
Terrain: **Parkland**

Length m **5,710**	Length l **5,070**
Par/SSS m **68/68**	Par/SSS l **70/70**
Rec m **65**	Rec l **64**
Par 3 m **2**	Par 3 l **2**
Par 5 m **0**	Par 5 l **0**

Signature Hole: Eighth, played form elevated tee to small green through arcade of birch trees and guarded by a deep faced bunker on right

Captain's Hole: Eighth

Times to Avoid: Open competition days

Clubhouse: Small well appointed club with bar. Catering available.

Condition: Always dry and playable – well manicured and speedy contoured greens.

Memorabilia: Jumpers

Wildlife: Deer, badgers, rabbits, hare, barn owls, buzzard, woodpeckers, red squirrels.

Location: Well signed in town. From Haugh of Urr take Dalbeattie Road, turn left just through 30 mph sign, second on left and course 150 yards on right.

Accommodation: Clonyard Country Hotel, Kippford; Imperial, Castle Douglas; Kings Head, Dalbeattie.

Lost ball: 4

Comments: Relaxed and challenging to all golfers, friendly with wonderful views.

Discount: Bunkered and tourist Board Gateway Pass

Clubs visiting: Contact Secretary

Caps visiting: Contact Secretary

C B BG CTR PG P

30 Crichton

Est: 1884

Tel: **01387 247894**

Bankend Road, Dumfries, DG1 4TH
Contact: **Claire Mullraney**
Email: **crichtongolf@hotmail.co.uk**
Website:
www.crichtongolfclub.limewebs.com
Terrain: **Parkland**

Length m **5,806**	Length l **5,400**
Par/SSS m **70/69**	Par/SSS l **72/71**
Rec m **64**	Rec l **70**
Par 3 m **4**	Par 3 l **4**
Par 5 m **2**	Par 5 l **4**

Signature Hole: Fifth, long PAR 3 to a green guarded by huge tree and bunkers. A great challenge.

Captain's Hole: Seventh, long PAR 4, tree lines which narrow the last 150 yards.

Times to Avoid: Saturday/Tuesday/Thursday.

Clubhouse: Large clubhouse with function room, full menu served daily from 11am – dark.

Condition: Excellent conditions with some of the fastest greens in the region.

Memorabilia: A range of clothing.

Wildlife: Birdlife, rabbits.

Location: Directly opposite Dumfries and Galloway Royal Infirmary.

Accommodation: Local hotels

Lost ball: 3

Comments: A challenging course

Fame: Sam Torrance, Andrew Coltart, Anders Fosbrand

Discount: Visit Scotland

Clubs visiting: Contact Secretary

Caps visiting: Yes. Contact Secretary

C B CH T CHR SHW CTR
PG P

---

31 New Galloway

Est: 1902

Tel: **01644 420737**

High Street, New Galloway, Dumfries and
Galloway, DG7 3RN
Contact: **N. E. White**
Email: **brown@nggc.co.uk**
Website: **www.nggc.co.uk**
Terrain: **Moorland**

Length m **5,006**	Length l **4,542**
Par/SSS m **68/67**	Par/SSS l **70/69**
Rec m **61**	
Par 3 m **3**	Par 3 l **4**
Par 5 m **0**	Par 5 l **2**

Signature Hole: Eighth, 367 yds PAR 4. Elevated tee then uphill over a gully and rock outcrop.

Captain's Hole: Third, 358 PAR 4. Needs a good drive over a wall at 170 yards.

Times to Avoid: Check with Sec.

Clubhouse: Licensed clubhouse with changing facilities

Condition: Immaculate greens and well tended fairways.

Memorabilia: Yes

Wildlife: Deer, pheasants, buzzards and red kite

Location: At the end of the main street, New Galloway

Accommodation: Ken Bridge Hotel, Cross Keys Hotel, Ken Mure Hotel

Lost ball: 2

Comments: Good test of golf on super greens with beautiful views – a hidden gem

Fame: Greg. Turner, Fred Olsen

Discount: D & G. Tourist Board

Clubs visiting: Contact Secretary

Caps visiting: Contact Secretary

C B BG CH T CHR SHW
CTR PG P

---

32 Castle Douglas

Est: 1905

Tel: **01556 502801**

Abercrombie Road, Castle Douglas,
Kirkcudbrightshire, DG7 1LN
Contact: **James Greenfield**
Email: **cdgolfclub@aol.com**
Website: **www.cdgolfclub.co.uk**
Terrain: **Parkland, one steep hill and views of the Galloway Hills.**

Length m **6,254**	Length l **5,548**
Par/SSS m **71/71**	Par/SSS l **72**
Par 3 m **4**	Par 3 l **4**
Par 5 m **2**	Par 5 l **4**

Signature Hole: Sixth, PAR 5, over 600 yards, one the country's longest holes.

Captain's Hole: First, PAR 3 to a small green offering a challenging opening.

Times to Avoid: Tuesdays and Thursdays after 3pm

Clubhouse: Good facilities, open from April to mid-October.

Condition: Good, but can be muddy after heavy rain

Wildlife: Birds of prey, including red kites. Occasional deer

Location: Half a mile from town clock, on left hand side of Abercromby Road, A713

Accommodation: Wide choice

Lost ball: 2

Comments: A friendly informal club which offers a real challenge to all golfers.

Discount: Gateway to Golf

Clubs visiting: Contact Secretary

Caps visiting: Courtesy of the Course

C B T CHR SHW CTR PG P

CTR Catering **PG** Putting Green **D** Driving **P** Practice **S** Pro-shop

justify the climb. Your jumbo driver will be out of the bag for the PAR 5 sixth which is one of the longest holes in Scotland at over 600 yards.

Three miles north of the fishing centre of Kirkcudbright on the A711 is the **33 Park of Tongland** golf course. Set in the Dee Valley the course, which is undergoing many improvements, offers stunning views and a relaxed, friendly atmosphere. Enjoy the fifth hole where the raised tee offers some of the best views and plays across a sloping fairway. For the members one of the favourite holes is the second where there is out-of-bounds to the right and a gully before the green.

Nine miles north-west of Kirkcudbright is the **34 Gatehouse of Fleet** golf course, which members claim is 'one of the most scenic and well maintained courses in s.w. Scotland'. Who are we to argue? Especially as the ninth hole is listed in Britain's 100 Extraordinary Golf Holes book. Despite this the Captain nominates the fourth as his favourite hole. It is a 322 yard PAR 4 where he says you 'miss the green at your peril'. You have been warned.

The authors have not been to this course and little information is available. **35 Wigtown** is Scotland's National Book Centre and a round of golf could be another reason to visit this corner of Scotland's south west. The course is described as a very pleasant nine holer and a good test to players of all abilities. Set in lush parkland half a mile from Wigtown centre the course 'is a haven for those seeking relaxing golf and a friendly atmosphere.' From the fourth tee there are magnificent views across the Solway Firth to the Lake District Hills.

If your tour takes you in this direction head south-west to **36 St Medan** at Monreith which is three miles south of Port William off the A747. A friendly welcome here and it is an ideal course for beginners and families as there are few restrictions. For non-golfers there are sea birds, otters and basking sharks and lovely wild flowers. The signature hole is the

33
Park of Tongland

Est: 1992

Tel: **01556 680226**

Tongland, Kirkcudbright, DG6 4NE
Contact: **Brian Thomson**
Email: **info@tonglandgolf.co.uk**
Website: **www.tonglandgolf.co.uk**
Terrain: **Parkland**

Length m **2,210**	Length l **1,748**
Par/SSS m **54/54**	Par/SSS l **54/54**
Rec m 25 (9 holes)	
Par 3 m 9	Par 3 l 9
Par 5 m 0	Par 5 l 0

Signature Hole: Fifth, 110 yards from a raised tee offering views across most of the course, with the fairways slopkng left to right.

Captain's Hole: Second, requires accurate tee shot to avoid o.o.b. to the right and across a dip in the fairway before the green.

Clubhouse: Comfortable with a full range of facilities

Condition: Good. Many improvements taking place

Memorabilia: Ball markers, polo shirts, hats.

Wildlife: Birdlife including birds of prey, housemartins and swallows. Deer, stoats and rabbits.

Location: Easily found in Tongland, three miles north of Kirkcudbright on the A711

Accommodation: Arden House Hotel, Tongland.

Lost ball: 4

Comments: Set in the Dee Valley the course offering stunning views in a friendly atmosphere.

Discount: 2for1, Green Fee Savers, Open Fairways Greenfree & Visit Scotland Golf Pass Scheme

Clubs visiting: Contact Secretary

Caps visiting: Free

C CH T PG D P S

34 Gatehouse of Fleet

Est: 1921

Tel: 01557 814766

Laurieston Road, Gatehouse of Fleet, DG7 2BE
Contact: **Steve Groome**
Email: **info@gatehousegolfclub.com**
Website: **www.gatehousegolfclub.com**
Terrain: **Parkland**

Length m **4,836**	Length l **4,836**
Par/SSS m **66/66**	Par/SSS l **66/66**
Rec m **63**	
Par 3 m **4**	Par 3 l **4**
Par 5 m **1**	Par 5 l **1**

Signature Hole: Ninth, PAR 3 Elevated tee down to green with back bunkers and o.o.b. over dyke on the right.

Captain's Hole: Fourth, 322 yard PAR 4 across the side of the course with forest to the right o.o.b. and a very undulating faiarway to a small green.

Times to Avoid: First Sunday of month April – October

Clubhouse: Warm and friendly with good facilities

Condition: Excellent, renowned for the greens, many slopes, original grass bunkers are features

Memorabilia: Yes, from Masonic Arms in Gatehouse of Fleet

Wildlife: Deer, kites, buzzards, estuary birds. Many species of birds in a number of local woodland nature reserves.

Location: Signposts in the town point out the Laurieston Road.

Accommodation: Many small hotels and B&Bs. in the town, including Murray Arms, Bank of Fleet and the Cally Hotel.

Lost ball: 2

Comments: The challenging nine-hole course is one of the most scenic and well maintained courses in s. w. Scotland.

Fame: A. J. Balfour (Prime Minister), William Whitelaw (US Ambassador), Jack White, Open Champion, Bernard Gallacher, Ryder Cup Captain

Discount: Yes

Clubs visiting: Contact Secretary

Caps visiting: Yes. Contact Secretary

> C B BG CH T CHR SHW CTR PG P

35 Wigtown and Bladnoch

Est. unknown

Tel: 01988 403 354

Lightlands Terrace, Wigtown, DG8 9DY
Website: **www.scottishgolfsouthwest.com**
Terrain: **Parkland**
Length **5462 yards**
Par/SSS **67/67**

DANGER
PLAYERS MUST NOT TEE OFF
FROM THE FIRST TEE
WHILST THERE ARE PEOPLE
ON THE 9th GREEN
PLAYERS MUST TAKE ALL REASONABLE STEPS
TO ENSURE THAT THE 1st AND 9th FAIRWAYS
ARE CLEAR BEFORE PLAYING OFF

36 St Medan

Est: 1905

Tel: 01988 700358

Monreith, Port William, Newton Stewart, DG8 8NJ
Contact: **Ronald Graham**
Email: **mail@stmedangolfclub.com**
Website: **www.stmedangolfclub.net**
Terrain: **Links**

Length m **4,520**	Length l **4,245**
Par/SSS m **64/64**	Par/SSS l **67/65**
Rec m **60**	Rec l **67**
Par 3 m **4**	Par 3 l **3**
Par 5 m **0**	Par 5 l **0**

Signature Hole: Fourth, elevated tee playing over a sleeper barricade at 200 yards. A good drive finishes on the green.

Times to Avoid: Wednesday and Friday afternoons

Clubhouse: Comfortable with views over the course and the Bay. Changing rooms, bar and limited catering available in summer

Condition: Excellent – open all year

Memorabilia: Ball markers, centenary book, jumpers and shirts

Wildlife: Sea birds, otters, basking sharks and wild flowers

Location: From A75 follow signs to Port William and Monreith via A47 and B7085

Accommodation: Check with Local Tourist Board

Lost ball: 2

Comments: Friendly and welcoming; ideal course for beginners and families, with few restrictions

Fame: In 1931 James Braid helped redesign some of the holes.

Discount: Bunkered

Clubs visiting: Contact Secretary

Caps visiting: Free to Club Secretaries

> C B CH T CHR SHW CTR PG P

fourth played from an elevated tee over a sleeper barricade at 200 yards. A good tee shot will finish on the green. How often have we told ourselves this?

The last course in this southern section of the area takes us to Portpatrick on the A77 south-west from Stranraer and the **37 Dinvin** course. Sitting above the picturesque fishing village it enjoys views of the Irish coastline and the Mull of Kintyre. The 18 hole 'Dunskey' course was established in 1903 and the nine-holer was created in 1912 from what had been the original 'ladies' course. It has been described in '*Golf World*' as 'The best holiday course in the south of Scotland.

The next part of this region worthy of our attention is across the southern uplands around Cumnock and Kilmarnock where the first course to be visited is the **38 Euchan** course at Sanquhar, just 440 yards from the A76 Dumfries-Kilmarnock road. This parkland course has a good clubhouse with bar and catering, changing rooms and shower facilities, while there is also a putting green and a practice area.

At Lochill on the A76 is the testing parkland course of **39 New Cumnock**, designed by Willie Fernie in 1901. Visitors are welcome at any time except Sundays before 4 pm. This great little course will test your shot-making to the full, and the score will normally depend on the short game.

Some 25 miles from Ayr on the A70 road to Edinburgh is the heathland course of **40 Muirkirk**. Established in 1991 this is another very scenic course with views of the 1,900 foot Cairn Table. It is also a course difficult to beat as the men's record is 70, two strokes above the par of 68. In addition to fine golf it also offers changing rooms and catering facilities. We feel a particular affinity to this lovely course as the difficult PAR 4 fifth hole is named 'McAdam's Stane', the only hole we have discovered to bear our family name. It seems that this hole is on the site where the famous road builder 'Tar McAdam' had his

37
Portpatrick-Dinvin

Est: 1914

Tel: **01776 810273**

Golf Course Road, Portpatrick, DG9 8TB
Contact: **The Secretary**
Email: **enquiries@portpatrickgolfclub.com**
Website: **www.portpatrickgolfclub.com**
Terrain: **Parkland**
Length m **3,008**
Par/SSS m **54/54**

| Par 3 m **9** | Par 3 l |
| Par 5 m **0** | Par 5 l |

Location: Situated in the town

C B BG CH T CHR SHW
CTR PG S

C Clubhouse **B** Bar **BG** Buggy **CH** Club Hire **T** Trolley **CHR** Changing Rooms **SHW** Showers

38
Sanquhar-Euchan

Est: 1894

Tel: **01659 58167**

Blackaddie Road, Sanquhar, Dumfriesshire, DG4 6JZ

Contact: **Ian MacFarlane**

Email: **tich@rossirene.fsnet.co.uk**

Website: **www.scottishgolfsouthwest.com**

Terrain: **Undulating parkland**

Length m **5,594**	Length l **5,178**
Par/SSS m **70/68**	Par/SSS l **74/74**
Rec m **64**	
Par 3 m **2**	Par 3 l **2**
Par 5 m **1**	Par 5 l **3**

Signature Hole: Second, long PAR 4 with slight dog-leg to right

Clubhouse: Gents/Ladies/Junior changing rooms, bar/meals by arrangement

Condition: Can be wet in spring

Wildlife: Birdlife

Location: Quarter of a mile from A76 Dumfries to Kilmarnock Road

Accommodation: Check with Tourist Information

Lost ball: 2

Comments: Good value

Discount: Bunkered

Clubs visiting: Contact Secretary

C B CHR SHW CTR PG P

39
New Cumnock

Est: 1902

Tel: **01290 338848**

Lochhill, Cumnock Road, Ayrshire, New Cumnock, KA18 4 BQ

Contact: **The Secretary**

Email: **newcumnockgolfclub@hotmail.co.uk**

Website: **www.newcumnockgolfclub.com**

Terrain: **Parkland**

Length m **4,804**	Length l **4,754**
Par/SSS m **65/66**	Par/SSS l **66/66**
Par 3 m **3**	Par 3 l **3**
Par 5 m **0**	Par 5 l **0**

Location: One mile west of New Cumnock

C B CHR CTR

40
Muirkirk

Est: 1991

Tel: **01290 660184**

'Southside', Furnace Road, Muirkirk, KA18 3QQ

Contact: **The Secretary**

Email: **bertbradford@ayrshire-precision.co.uk**

Website: **www.scottishgolfsouthwest.com**

Terrain: **Heathland**

Length m **5,380**

Par/SSS m **68/66**

Par 3 m **2**	Par 3 l **2**
Par 5 m **0**	Par 5 l **0**

Location: 13 miles off the M74 at Junction 12 on A70 towards Ayr

Comments: Course kept in first Class condition and catering for golfers of all abilities.

Fame: Catriona Matthew, Rory Bremner and many rugby internationals.

Discount: Yes

Clubs visiting: Contact Secretary

Caps visiting: Yes

C B T CHR SHW CTR

St Medan Golf Course

first tar kiln and became the starting point for modern roads the world over. Take time for a chat to the greenkeeper 'Wee' Strickland, after whom the second hole is named.

41 Doon Valley, Patna (a few miles south of Ayr on the A713) offers a true example of the friendly atmosphere found at many of the smaller local courses in Scotland. Although it boasts little more than 100 members the course has well maintained greens and fairways and offers outstanding views of the surrounding countryside. The terrain is undulating parkland and spreads across the hillside of the Doon Valley, where a striking feature is Gilmours Gulley which comes into play on a number of holes. There is a small clubhouse with changing rooms, catering and bar.

Getting away for a while from the rolling country-side of rural south Ayrshire try the town centre course at **42 Maybole**, (nine miles south of Ayr on the A77) set in the town's Memorial Park. There are a few baby hills on the undulating fairways, nothing to cause too much of a problem, but the small, well-protected greens offer a challenge to all standards of golfers. Close by the course there is a swimming pool and bowling green so there is much to do for those members of the party who have yet to discover the glories of golf.

A lovely diversion now taking the A77 west towards the Ayrshire coast and the glorious **43 Turnberry Resort** with its outstanding view of Ailsa Craig, a little island made famous by the coverage of championship golf on TV. In 2001 this famous golfing and hotel centre added the nine-hole Arran course to its two 18 holers. This is a typical Scottish links type course where the undulating greens, tight tee shots, pot bunkers and thick rough make it a great training ground for the Turnberry Golf Academy. With six professionals there is always guidance on hand for those little swing problems. The signature hole and most talked about on the course, is the PAR 4 fifth. At 425 yards it presents plenty of challenges. It is tight

41
Doon Valley-Patna

Est: 1927

Tel: **01292 531607**

1 Hillside, Patna, Ayrshire, KA6 7JT
Contact: **Hugh Johnstone, MBE**
Email: **david.brown@east-ayrshire.gov.uk**
Website: **www.east-ayrshire.gov.uk**
Terrain: **Parkland**

Length m **5,850**	Length l **5,152**
Par/SSS m **70/70**	Par/SSS l **70/72**
Rec m **69**	
Par 3 m **2**	Par 3 l **2**
Par 5 m **2**	Par 5 l **2**

Times to Avoid: Weekends

Clubhouse: Changing facilities with toilet and showers for ladies and gents

Condition: Good in summer, variable in winter

Wildlife: Varied birdlife

Location: On A713 Ayr to Castle Douglas Road, ten miles south of Ayr

Accommodation: Kirkton Inn, Dalrymple

Lost ball: 2

Comments: Leisurely course with no hassle

C B CHR SHW PG P

C Clubhouse **B** Bar **BG** Buggy **CH** Club Hire **T** Trolley **CHR** Changing Rooms **SHW** Showers

42
Maybole

Est: Unknown

Tel: **01655 889770**

Memorial Park, Maybole, Ayrshire, KA19 7DX
Contact: **The Secretary**
Email: **golf@south-ayrshire.gov.uk**
Website: **www.golfsouthayrshire.com**
Terrain: **Parkland**
Length m **5,380**
Par/SSS m **66/66**
Par 3 m **3**
Par 5 m **0**
Location: Nine miles south of Ayr on the A77

C CHR PG

43
Arran Course – Turnberry

Est: 2001

Turnberry Resort, Maidens Road, Turnberry,
Ayrshire, KA26 9LT
Contact: **Ricky Hill**
Email: **turnberrytee-
times@luxurycollection.com**
Website: **www.turnberryresort.co.uk**
Terrain: **Links**

Length: m **3,992**	Length l **3,730**
Par/SSS: m **62**	Par/SSS l **62**
Par 3 m **5**	Par 3 l **5**
Par 5 m **0**	Par 5 l **0**

Signature Hole: Fifth 425 yds PAR 4. A hole on
the original Arran course when it was an 18
holer. Tight off the tee, double dog let and three
bunkers around the green.

Times to Avoid: None

Clubhouse: Luxurious

Memorabilia: Everything Turnberry available,
from clothes to jewellery

Condition: Outstanding

Wildlife: Seabirds

Location: Follow the A77, then two miles past
Kirkoswald take the right-hand turn signposted
Turnberry.

Accommodation: You don't need to ask!

Clubs visiting: Contact professional

**C B BG CH T CHR SWH
CTR PG D P S**

Maybole Golf Course

off the tee, there is an S shaped double dog-leg and three bunkers protecting the green. Just making it to the sixth with par on the card would be a triumph in itself.

A couple of miles from the centre of Ayr the **44 Roodlea** Family Golf Centre boasts a tight nine-holer measuring just short of 3,800 yards and a PAR of 34. In addition to the course the Golf Academy has a 17 bay floodlit driving range, an all grass short game area, a golf coaching academy, pro-shop and café. This a flat parkland course where the greatest challenge is on the PAR 3 ninth, played downhill through a stand of trees and with a burn running down the right hand side.

The final three courses in the south-west before crossing to the far side of the River Clyde are Caprington, Auchenharvie and North Gailes.

45 Caprington is a municipal course just one and a half miles south of Kilmarnock on the B7038 offering a mixture of links and parkland terrain. Although a little shorter than many nine-holers at 3,462 yards and a PAR of 60 it does not present too many problems, with generous fairways and a few hills. Visitors are not allowed on the course on Saturdays, but they can always relax at the bar or the pro shop.

Should you be looking for a one stop golfing break for the whole family you might do worse than **46 North Gailes**, Marine Drive, Irvine. Situated just off the A78 this is a complete leisure centre offering gym, spa, beauty zone, a 27 bay floodlit driving range and professional golf tuition in addition to the challenging course. The attractive signature hole is the sixth with a tee shot through a narrow gap in pine trees and a final approach over a large pond to a double green.

While in this area of North Ayrshire make time for a visit to **47 Auchenharvie** golf course, also situated close to the A78 on Moorpark Road West, Stevenston. This open, parkland course with water features was opened in 1981 and although a nine-holer it can also be played

44
Roodlea

Est: Changed from 18 holes to 9 holes in 2011.

Tel: **01292 570 727**

Ayr Family Golf Centre, Ayr, KA6 6EP
Contact: **Barry Wortley**
Email: **golfpro@ayrgolfcentre.co.uk**
Website: **www.ayrgolfcentre.co.uk**
Terrain: **Parkland**
Length **3,764**
Par/SSS **64/64**
Par 3 **4**
Par 5 **0**

Signature Hole: The PAR 3 ninth is an intimidating hole with a downhill tee shot through trees with a burn down the right hand side.

Clubhouse: The Golf Academy offers full facilities

Condition: Good

Location: Past Dobbies Garden Centre on the A70 heading towards Coylton.

Accommodation: Hotels and B & B's. in Ayr

Comments: Well drained offering all-year round golf

Discounts: Available for group bookings and special offers during the winter.

C B CTR PG D P S

45 Caprington

Est: Unknown

Tel: **01563 521915/554061**

Ayr Road, Caprington, Kilmarnock, KA1 4UW
Contact: **The Secretary**
Email: **caprington.golf@east-ayrshire.gov.uk**
Website: **www.east-ayrshire.gov.uk**
Terrain: **Parkland**
Length m **3,462**
Par/SSS m **60/60**
Par 3 m **6**
Par 5 m **0**
Location: On the B7038 Ayr Road at the edge of town on right.

C CHR PG P

46 North Gailes

Est: 2002

Tel: **01294 316090**

Marine Drive, Irvine, KA11 5AE
Contact: **Douglas McEwan**
Email: **reception@northgailes.co.uk**
Website: **www.northgailes.co.uk**
Terrain: **Parkland with links features**

Length m **4,486**	Length l **4,486**
Par/SSS m **65/62**	Par/SSS l **66/62**
Par 3 m **4**	Par 3 l **4**
Par 5 m **1**	Par 5 l **2**

Signature Hole: Sixth, tee shot through a narrow gap in pine trees with a final approach over a large pond to a double green

Times to Avoid: Saturday 8–11am

Clubhouse: Very good facilities

Condition: Yet to mature

Wildlife: Birdlife, foxes and ducks

Location: Adjacent to A78 and neighbours with Glasgow Gailes and Dundonald Links

Accommodation: Gailes Hotel

Comments: Challenging course with easy walking and superb clubhouse

Fame: Bill Lockie, John McTear, Ross Aitken (PGA pros.)

C B T CHR SHW PG D S

47 Auchenharvie

Est: 1981

Tel: **01294 603103**

Moor Park Road West, Stevenston, Ayrshire, KA20 3HU
Contact: **The Secretary**
Email: **info@kaleisure.com**
Website: **www.kaleisure.com**
Terrain: **Parkland**

Length m **5,203**	Length l **4,958**
Par/SSS m **66/66**	Par/SSS l **69/66**
Rec m **n/a**	Rec l
Par 3 m **3**	Par 3 l **3**
Par 5 m **0**	Par 5 l **1**

Location: On the road between Saltcoats and Stevenston

C B CH CTR PG D

as 18 holes using different tee positions on the second nine. An added facility is an 18 bay driving range.

Our journey now takes us north across the Clyde to the wild beauty of the Kintyre Peninsula, not far from the fishing centre of Campbeltown. **48 The Pans** course at Machrihanish is the junior partner of the world famous links course close to the southern end of the Mull of Kintyre. It offers a proper links challenge with tight fairways and a number of demanding greens, including the first with its crown green sending the putt in unexpected directions.

The next part of the tour heads further north into some rugged scenery and outstanding nine-hole opportunities. The furthest west of this group of courses is **49 Carradale**, 15 miles north of Campbeltown just off the A842. This is a beautiful inland course which is not too demanding from the yellow tees. See how you get on with the PAR 3 signature seventh played from an elevated tee with o.o.b. to the right and left. For added interest wild goats can occasionally be seen here, possibly appreciated by the famous Scottish Ladies amateur player, Belle Robertson, unquestionably Scotland's finest-ever Ladies' amateur player – the oldest member (at 50) to represent the British and Irish team in the Curtis Cup – winning on US soil.

The fishing port of **50 Tarbert,** world famous for its Loch Fyne kippers, is situated at the end of the Loch where it enters the Sound of Bute. The lovely course is a mile to the west of the town off the A83. This is a hilly and wooded heathland course with streams crossing four of the fairways adding to the challenge and interest. The course record is 62, one stroke less than the SSS.

If it's wonderful views you hanker for then head quickly (well, as fast as you can, via the short ferry crossing to Portavadie) to the **51 Kyles of Bute**, at Kames, Tighnabruaich, a course popular with many TV personalities. On this peaceful, inland course you will find little to pressure your game although the

48
The Pans, Machrihanish

Est: 1890

Tel: **01586 810277**

Machrihanish, Argyll, PA28 6PT
Email: **secretary@machgolf.com**
Website: **www.machgolf.com**
Terrain: **Links**
Length: **4752 yards**
Par/SSS: **68/64**
Par 3s **3**
Par 5s **1**

Signature Hole: First. A fairly straightforward 184 yard PAR three made a lot more difficult by the crown green.

Clubhouse: Full use of all the facilities of the Machrihanish Club.

Condition: Fair, can get soggy following heavy rain in the winter.

Location: Part of the famous Machrihanish Club

Discounts: Winter rates at less than £10 for a day ticket.

C B CH T CHR SHW CTR
PG D P S

SLOW PLAY

Slow play spoils the game. Be courteous and allow faster games to play through.

C Clubhouse B Bar BG Buggy CH Club Hire T Trolley CHR Changing Rooms SHW Showers

49
Carradale

Est: 1906

Tel: **01583 431321**

Carradale, Argyll, East Kintyre, PA28 6QT
Contact: **Dr R. J. Abernethy**
Email: **margaretrichardson1977@live.co.uk**
Website: **www.carradalegolf.com**
Terrain: **Moorland**

Length m **4,884**	Length l **3,929**
Par/SSS m **65/64**	Par/SSS l **66/63**
Par 3 m **4**	Par 3 l **4**
Par 5 m **0**	Par 5 l **0**

Signature Hole: Seventh, 240 yd PAR 3 with OB right and left. Played from an elevated tee.

Times to Avoid: Saturdays

Clubhouse: Basic with mens and ladies changing rooms and toilets. Lockers.

Condition: Lovely fairways, good greens.

Memorabilia: Yes, including holdalls and centenary whisky.

Wildlife: Wild goats, birdlife.

Location: 15 miles north of Campbeltown and East Kintyre, facing Arran.

Accommodation: Carradale Hotel, Dunvalanree Guest House, Kiloran House. The Glen.

Lost ball: 1

Comments: Beautiful scenery in good condition and not too demanding from yellow tees.

Fame: Belle Robertson

Discount: Bunkered

Clubs visiting: Contact Secretary

Caps visiting: Courtesy of the course

C T CHR PG P

50
Tarbert

Est: Unknown

Tel: **01546 606896**

Kilberry Road, Tarbert, Loch Fynne, Argyll, PA29 6XX
Contact: **The Secretary**
Email: **secretary@tarbertgolfclub.org.uk**
Website: **www.tarbertgolfclub.org.uk**
Terrain: **Hilly heathland**
Length m **4,460**

Par/SSS m **66/63**	
Par 3 m **3**	
Par 5 m **0**	

Location: One mile off A83 south of Tarbert

HELP THE GREENKEEPER

Please ....
repair pitch marks,
replace divots
and rake bunkers.

51
Kyles of Bute

Est: 1906

Tel: **01700 811603**

The Moss, Kames, Tighnabruaich, PA21 2BE
Contact: **Dr Jeremy Thomson**
Website: **www.kylesofbutegolfclub.co.uk**
Terrain: **Heath and heather**

Length m **4,814**	Length l **4,010**
Par/SSS m **66/64**	Par/SSS l **66/66**
Rec m **62**	
Par 3 m **3**	Par 3 l **3**
Par 5 m **0**	Par 5 l **0**

Signature Hole: Ninth, PAR 3 from an elevated tee with outstanding views

Captain's Hole: Seventh, PAR 4 from a high tee down to a sloping fairway and a small green. Wonderful views.

Times to Avoid: Sunday morning

Clubhouse: Unattended clubhouse with clubrooom, kitchen, changing rooms.

Condition: Variable according to weather. Good greens

Memorabilia: Ball markers

Wildlife: Deer, hare, varied birds, including buzzards, kestrel, grouse, pheasant, lapwing and curlew.

Location: From the B8000 to Tighnabruaich turn right at the shore to Kames, crossroad turn right.

Accommodation: Kames Hotel, Royal Hotel, Tighnabruaich.

Lost ball: 1

Comments: Peaceful, and with no pressure

Fame: Various TV personalities

Discount: Bunkered

Clubs visiting: Contact Secretary

C CH T

views can be distracting. This is particularly true on the PAR 3 ninth played from an elevated tee and also on the captain's favourite hole, the sixth, where there is a panoramic view from the tee with a long downhill fairway to a bunkered green.

Situated six miles south of Dunoon on the A815 is the interesting hilltop moorland course of **52 Innellan** with outstanding views over the Firth of Clyde. Visitors are welcome at all times, except after 4 pm on Mondays, although it is very possible that the friendly bar will be open. Watch for the 'Rubicon' which as its name suggests is played across a gorge at 250 yards.

A little further north lies the **53 Blairmore and Strone** golf course, seven miles from Dunoon in the village of Strone. Take the A815 and then the A880. Designed by James Braid, Scotland's most celebrated golf course architect, and opened in 1896 this course has breathtaking views of Loch Long and the Firth of Clyde. The terrain is a mixture of hills and parkland. In 2007 it was host to the Firth of Clyde Trophy, the oldest inter-community competition in the world and inaugurated two years after the founding of the course. If no members are in attendance post your green fees to the honesty box.

The final part of the tour of the south-west region takes us firmly into the Highlands where there are superb hidden golfing diamonds in rough landscapes. At **54 Lochgilphead** there is a wee terror of a course situated on the Blarbuie Road at the rear of the famous Argyll and Bute hospital. Described as a parkland course it nevertheless embraces at least one steep hill at the PAR 3 third which plays far longer than its 114 yards (from the yellow tees). Both fairways and greens are in good condition and the clubhouse offers snacks and soup during the summer months.

Further north along Loch Fyne lies the parkland course of **55 Inveraray**, one mile south of the immaculately planned town at the heart of Clan Campbell. Described by the secretary as 'a nine-hole gem of the west coast', it is both scenic and testing but

52
Innellan

Est: 1891

Tel: **01369 830242**

Knockamillie Road, Innellan, Argyll, PA23 7SG
Contact: **The Secretary**
Email: **innellangolfclub@btconnect.com**
Website: **www.innellangolfclub.co.uk**
Terrain: **Hilltop moorland**
Length m **4,686**
Par/SSS **64/64**

Location: Four miles south of Dunoon on coastal road to Innellan Pier

C B CH T CHR CTR P

C Clubhouse **B** Bar **BG** Buggy **CH** Club Hire **T** Trolley **CHR** Changing Rooms **SHW** Showers

53
Blairmore and Strone

Est: 1896

Tel: **01369 840676**

High Road, Strone, Dunoon, PA23 8JJ
Contact: **The Secretary**
Email: **info@blairmoregc.co.uk**
Website: **www.blairmore.co.uk**
Terrain: **Hilly**

Length m **3,792**	Length l **3,686**
Par/SSS m **62/61**	Par/SSS l **62/62**
Par 3 m **5**	Par 3 l **5**
Par 5 m **0**	Par 5 l

Location: Seven miles from Dunoon

54
Lochgilphead

Est: 1892

Tel: **01546 510383**

Blarbuie Road, Lochgilphead, Argyll, PA31 8LE
Contact: **Bob Foyle**
Website: **www.lochgilphead-golf.com**
Terrain: **Parkland**

Length m **4,518**	Length l **3,926**
Par/SSS m **64/63**	Par/SSS l **66/65**
Rec m **58**	Rec l **65**
Par 3 m **4**	Par 3 l **4**
Par 5 m **0**	Par 5 l **2**

Times to Avoid: Saturday and Sunday mornings.

Clubhouse: Changing rooms and toilets with bar and catering at weekends.

Condition: Very good

Memorabilia: Yes

Wildlife: Deer and birds of prey

Location: Follow signposts from town centre

Accommodation: Cairnbaan Hotel, Burnsies Restaurant

Lost ball: 1

Comments: Fair test of golf in a picturesque setting.

Fame: Sir Tom Farmer

Discount: Bunkered and Fore

Clubs visiting: Contact Secretary

Caps visiting: Contact Secretary

C B CH T CHR CTR P S

55
Inveraray

Est: 1893

Tel: **01499 302079**

North Cromalt, Inveraray, Argyll, PA32 8XT
Contact: **Calum Morrison**
Terrain: **Parkland**

Length m **5,628**	Length l **4,860**
Par/SSS m **70/69**	Par/SSS l 70/70
Rec m **69**	
Par 3 m **4**	Par 3 l **4**
Par 5 m **1**	Par 5 l **2**

Signature Hole: Seventh, dog-leg to left. Tee shot is played through narrow gap in trees. Approach shot to green with Loch Fyne and surrounding hills as backdroop.

Captain's Hole: Fifth, over the pond. Position must be accurate on every shot.

Times to Avoid: Sundays

Clubhouse: Small portakabin with seating and drinks available.

Condition: Good

Memorabilia: Balls, ball markers, pitch repairers.

Location: Signposted just south of town on A83 Campbeltown road.

Accommodation: George Hotel, Argyll Hotel.

Lost ball: 2

Comments: A nine-hole gem of the west coast. Scenic, testing but not too tiring.

Fame: Ally McCoist and Russell Weir (Cowal Golf Club pro).

Discount: Bunkered 2 for 1

C CH T CHR

Lochgoilhead Golf Club

not too tiring. Scottish football star and TV personality Ally McCoist must think so for he has been seen on the course as has Russell Weir, the Cowal Golf Club professional. The sensible lay-out encourages bold tee-shots and the signature hole is the terrific dog-leg seventh where the drive is played through a narrow gap in the trees. The approach to the green has Loch Fyne and surrounding hills as a backdrop.

Not far away as the crow flies but a considerable distance by road is **56 Lochgoilhead,** approached by a six mile single track road from the Rest-and-Be-Thankful pass. Take the A83 and then the B828. Situated in the Loch Lomond and Trossachs National Park this is a scenic course following the head of the Loch before crossing over the River Goil. Although this is not a course for big hitters there are plenty of problems for wayward shots. As part of the Drimsynie Hotel and leisure complex there are hotel, restaurant and catering facilities on site and many leisure activities.

At **57 Dalmally** on the A85 a couple of miles to the west of the town is a picturesque flat parkland course bounded by the River Orchy to the north and over-looked by mighty Ben Cruachan, the 'Hollow Mountain'. In good condition it offers many water hazards and 14 greenside bunkers. It is usually fairly quiet and peaceful and local wildlife includes birds of prey, herons, otters and pine martin. The signature third hole is an attractive 175 yard PAR 3 with a 140 yard carry over the river that can be daunting for beginners – although rewarding for the more-capable golfer.

Further north-west on the A85, and just 12 miles from Oban, is the 4,510 yard inland course of **58 Taynuilt**. This challenging parkland course, located close to the foot of Cruachan, is surrounded by majestic scenery and has lovely views up Loch Etive. The famous amateur player and secretary of the R and A, Sir Michael Bonallack, opened the course in 1987. The PAR 3 eighth is the captain's favourite with a difficult tee shot through a tree lined fairway. However,

56
Lochgoilhead

Est: Unknown

Tel: **01301 703247**

Lochgoilhead, Argyll, PA24 8AD
Contact: **The Secretary**
Email: **info@argyllholidays.com**
Website: **www.argyllholidays.com**
Terrain: **Inland**
Length m **3,766**
Par/SSS m **60/60**
Par 3 m **6**
Par 5 m **0**

Location: North of Lochgoilhead, off Rest-and-Be-Thankful road.

C B CH CHR CTR PG

57
Dalmally

Est: 1987

Tel: **01838 200487**

Old Saw Mill, Dalmally, PA33 1AE
Contact: **R. Johnston**
Email: **dalmallygc@dsl.pipex.com**
Website: **www.dalmallygolfclub.co.uk**
Terrain: **Flat parkland**

Length m **4,168**	Length l **4,230**
Par/SSS m **64/63**	Par/SSS l **65/65**
Rec m **62**	Rec l **68**
Par 3 m **4**	Par 3 l **4**
Par 5 m **0**	Par 5 l **1**

Signature Hole: Third, picturesque drive over River Orchy

Captain's Hole: Third

Clubhouse: All facilities available

Condition: Good

Memorabilia: Yes

Wildlife: Birds of prey, herons, rabbits, otters, pine martin

Location: Road sign at joint entrance Strathorchy B & B

Accommodation: Craig Royston B & B, Strathorchy B & B

Lost ball: 2

Comments: Usually fairly quiet and peaceful

Fame: Clive Anderson, Jamie McGregor

Clubs visiting: Contact Secretary

C B CH T CTR

58
Taynuilt

Est: 1987

Tel: **01866 822429**

Taynuilt, Argyll, PA35 1JH
Contact: **Murray Sim**
Email: **jeremy.church@virgin.net**
Website: **www.taynaultgolfclub.co.uk**
Terrain: **Parkland**

Length m **4,510**	Length l **4,510**
Par/SSS m **64/63**	Par/SSS l **64/67**
Rec m **62**	
Par 3 m **4**	Par 3 l **4**
Par 5 m **0**	Par 5 l **0**

Signature Hole: Fourth, 373 yard with ditch, fairway views over Loch Etive and slopes to a green a sea level.

Captain's Hole: Eighth, PAR 3 with difficult tee shot with trees on both sides of green.

Times to Avoid: Sundays and Tuesday mid-day/

Condition: Good

Wildlife: Seabirds and ducks.

Location: Through Taynuilt village over railway, turn left onto course.

Accommodation: Robin's Nest tea room. Local accommodation.

Comments: A quiet, friendly, scenic course

Fame: Michael Bonallack opened the course

Discount: Green Fee Savers

Clubs visiting: Contact Secretary

Caps visiting: Yes

T P

our friend David Howitt says that the ninth is one of the best holes that he has ever played – anywhere!

Our final course in the South West is the **59 The Links at Eriska** golf course belonging to the Isle of Eriska Hotel, (take the A828 north at Connel) where visitors are welcome to both the course and other facilities. These include trolley hire, club hire, changing rooms, putting green, driving range and teaching academy as well as the hotel catering. Recently upgraded from six holes to nine it is both scenic and beautiful. The signature hole is the third, a 350 yard PAR 4 which is a dog-leg left to a well bunkered green. Doubtless Sir Sean Connery loved the bridge-approach road and the hospitality of this fabulous setting when he stayed there during the making of '*Entrapment*' – co-starring Catherine Zeta Jones. David Howitt tells me 'I was actually there whilst 20th Century Fox were making the film and I met the great man as he emerged alone from the imposing doorway before breakfast – sniffing the air like a venerable moose – and wishing me 'good morning' in that inimitable accent'.

59
The Links at Eriska

Est: 2002 (upgraded)

Tel: **01631 720802**

Isle of Eriska Hotel, Ledaig, Isle of Eriska, Argyll, PA37 1SD
Contact: **The Secretary**
Email: **spa@eriska-hotel.co.uk**
Website: **www.eriska-hotel.co.uk**
Terrain: **Parkland**
Length m **3,116 (6 holes)**
Par/SSS m **44/44**

Par 3 m **4**	Par 3 l **4**
Par 5 m **0**	Par 5 l

Signature Hole: Third, 350 yards PAR 4. Dog-leg left to a well bunkered green

Clubhouse: Yes

Location: North of Oban on A82

Accommodation: Isle of Eriska Hotel

C B CH T CHR CTR PG D P

Dalbeatie Golf Course

Doon Valley Golf Course, Patna

HIGHLAND

Argyll, Inverness-shire, Ross-shire, Sutherland, Caithness

The Highland region of Scotland covers the whole of the extensive counties of Inverness-shire, Ross-shire, Sutherland and Caithness and a tiny chunk of northern Argyll. It is vast, covering some 38,000 square miles and hundreds of miles of wild coastline. A glance at the map will show that it is largely 'untamed', with very few roads along the west and rather difficult journeys linking east to west.

Fortunately it is richly endowed with fine nine-hole golf courses, even if getting from one to another sometimes involves extensive travelling, much of it on twisty single track roads, and journeys from the west to the east to make a little progress north. Please do not be put off, it will be richly rewarding experience through dramatic and wild scenery to equal anything you may see anywhere in the word.

The courses are also wonderfully varied including some fine links, parkland, heathland and inland courses. In other words there is something to delight and challenge even the most demanding golfer.

In the absence of a logical route to embrace all 17 of these varied and exciting courses we have selected a journey from the south, travelling north to Durness, the most northerly golf course in Britain, and then heading south once again down the east coast taking in some of the Great Glen and Speyside courses.

This journey starts at Ballachulish where a ferry carried traffic across the Loch Leven rapids for nearly 250 years until it was eventually replaced by a bridge in 1975. The **60 Dragon's Tooth** golf course, named after the dramatic hill which towers over the course, is one of the new courses in Scotland designed by Robin Hiseman to take full advantage of the natural contours in the land. There are a number of challenging holes including the PAR 3 ninth played across a burn and through a stand of trees to a small green close to the

60
Dragon's Tooth

Est: Unknown

Tel: **01855 811695**

Ballachulish House Hotel, Ballachulish, Argyll, PH49 4JX
Contact: **The Secretary**
Email: **clubhouse@dragonstooth.co.uk**
Website: **www.dragonstooth.co.uk**
Terrain: **Parkland**

Length m **5,038**	Length l **4,406**
Par/SSS m **68/68**	Par/SSS l **68/68**
Par 3 m 3	Par 3 l 3
Par 5 m 1	Par 5 l 1

Clubhouse: Comfortable with good facilities

Condition: Good

Location: Three miles from Glencoe and 12 miles from Fort William

Accommodation: Ballahulish House, Ballachulish Hotel

Lost ball: 3

Discount: Contact Secretary

Caps visiting: Contact Secretary

C B CH T CHR CTR PG P

clubhouse. During 2012 a great deal of work was carried out including the addition of a further nine tees, making this a nine hole – 18 tee course.

61 Traigh Golf Course was described by the *Scotsman* newspaper as 'probably the most beautifully sited nine-hole golf course in the world.' Traigh (pronounced 'try') means 'beach' in Gaelic and a series of sandy beaches run alongside the course, with glorious views to the inner Hebridean islands of Eigg and Rum and the Cuillins of Skye. Find it two miles north of Arisaig on the A830 Fort William to Mallaig road. Well-maintained and offering a true links challenge the course has attracted a number of famous names including Ronan Rafferty. Wildlife in the area includes otters, seals and red deer.

Another superbly situated course also overlooking hill and loch, although not as manicured as some of the nine-hole Highland courses, is the beachside parkland course of **62 Lochcarron** situated on the A896 from Strathcarron station. There are 11 tees on this short but demanding course which offers a real challenge to all abilities of golfers, especially when the wind blows in from the loch. The fourth plays across the main road and demands some care which adds to the enjoyment, while several of the five holes to the north of the road play around an ancient church. It is open throughout the year with clubhouse facilities available during the summer season.

Along this stretch of the west coast of Scotland everything is so beautiful that it really stretches the superlatives, for every corner opens up another wonderful view. After playing Lochcarron, and as a diversion from the rigours of golf, it is worth taking a drive over the Bealach na Ba to Applecross. This is undoubtedly one of the most dramatic roads in Scotland with wonderful views in every direction but especially to the west and the islands of Scalpay, Skye and Raasay. Do stop at Applecross for a meal, it is a treat not to be missed.

Yet another course which, quite reasonably claims

61 Traigh

Est: 1985

Tel: **01687 450337**

Traigh, Arisaig, Inverness-shire, PH39 4NW
Contact: **Bill Henderson**
Website: **www.traighgolf.co.uk**
Terrain: **Seaside links**

Length m **4,912**	Length l **4,206**
Par/SSS m **68/65**	Par/SSS l **68/65**
Par 3 m **4**	Par 3 l **4**
Par 5 m **2**	Par 5 l **2**

Signature Hole: Fifth, PAR 3, Tee shot over the Atlantic to a small green

Captain's Hole: Fifth

Times to Avoid: Sundays 1–5 pm

Clubhouse: Small

Condition: Improving

Memorabilia: Ball markers

Wildlife: Seabirds, otters, seals and red deer

Location: By the beautiful white sands of Traigh

Accommodation: Cnoc na Faire Hotel, Arisaig

Lost ball: 5

Comments: Oustanding views of inner Hebrides

Fame: Ronan Rafferty, Mark MacGee

Clubs visiting: Contact Secretary

C CH

62
Lochcarron

Est: 1908

Tel: **01599 577219**

Lochcarron, Strathcarron, Ross-shire, IV54 8YS
Contact: **Gerry Arscott**
The Secretary: **Contact name**
Email: **info@lochcarrongolfclub.co.uk**
Website: **www.lochcarrongolfclub.co.uk**
Terrain: **Parkland**

Length m **3,575**	Length l **3,575**
Par/SSS m **60/60**	Par/SSS l **60/60**
Rec m **58**	
Par 3 m **6**	Par 3 l **6**
Par 5 m **0**	Par 5 l **0**

Signature Hole: First, 210 yards PAR 3 'Johnny's Seat'. One of the trickiest PAR 3s in Scotland

Captain's Hole: Ninth, PAR 3 176 yards. 'Bunker'. Beautiful view from tee looking over the Loch to Attadale

Times to Avoid: Saturdays (Club competitions)

Clubhouse: Unlicensed. Full catering with hot and cold food and seafood. Ladies and Gents changing rooms.

Condition: Can be wet

Memorabilia: Jumpers

Wildlife: Otters, eagles, red deer, sea birds

Location: On the A890 to junction near Strathcarron station, then A896

Accommodation: Check with tourist information

Lost ball: 5

Clubs visiting: By negotiation

Caps visiting: Yes

C CH T CHR CTR

Lochcarron Golf Course

to be in one of the most wonderful parts of the west coast is **63 Gairloch**, situated on the A832 about a mile south of the village, with two churches featuring in the scenery. The views south and west are quite stunning, but do not get distracted for with a number of fairways crossing each other a shout of 'fore' can see half the players ducking for cover. A friendly clubhouse offers catering during the season, with changing rooms, club and trolley hire and a range of memorabilia. Watch out for varied bird life including the occasional sea eagle, and other wildlife can include seals, minke whales, porpoise, dolphin and red and roe deer.

Heading back onto the A832 and then left at the junction with the A835 the road heads for the historic fishing port of **64 Ullapool**, home to one of the newer nine-hole courses in the Highlands, opened by Prince Andrew, the most famous royal golfer, in the spring of 1998. This is sometimes confused for an 18 hole course, for while there are just nine greens there are 18 tees, making for an interesting second round. The course is laid out to the north of the town along the banks of Loch Broom and mixes gorse with open and grassy verdure. Extensive views carry the eye from Loch Broom to the Summer Isles. The signature hole is the PAR 3 second played from an elevated tee with a river feature and views over the village, while the Captain's favourite is the ninth a PAR 4 straight forward hole with a 'devilish' green. Par for the men is 70 with a stroke index of 67 so there is a real challenge. The course is within walking distance of the village.

Situated on the north-west coast on the A838 **65 Durness** is the most northerly course on the British Isles mainland overlooking the beach and the wild Atlantic ocean, which explains why seals, porpoises, and otters can all be seen around the course and, when we played, a flock of sheep and their lambs. These are only allowed on the course for four weeks in the spring. It offers relaxed but challenging golf in peaceful, picturesque surroundings and is unusual

63
Gairloch

Est: 1898

Tel: **01445 712407**

Gairloch, Ross-shire, IV21 2BE
Contact: **The Secretary**
Email: **gairlochgolfclub@hotmail.co.uk**
Website: **www.gairlochgolfclub.co.uk**
Terrain: **Links**

Length m **4,108**	Length l **3,665**
Par/SSS m **62/62**	Par/SSS l **62/62**
Rec m **62**	
Par 3 m **6**	Par 3 l **6**
Par 5 m **1**	Par 5 l **1**

Times to Avoid: Competition mornings

Clubhouse: Refreshments, bar and changing rooms

Condition: Well maintained

Memorabilia: Yes

Wildlife: Varied bird-life including occasional sea eagle, seals, minke whales, porpoise, dolphin, red and roe deer.

Location: From south, on A832 1km after cattle grid, course on left. From north on A832 1½km after cattle grid on right after cemetery.

Accommodation: Old Inn, Gairloch

Comments: Short but demanding and is situated in one the most beautiful parts of the west coast.

Fame: Willie Fernie, designer of Royal Troon and Open winner in 1883.

Clubs visiting: Contact Secretary

Caps visiting: Contact Secretary

C B CH T CHR CTR S

64 Ullapool

Est: 1998

Tel: 01854 613323

North Road, Morefield, Ullapool, IV26 2TH
Contact: **Alan Paterson**
Email: **info@ullapool-golf.co.uk**
Website: **www.ullapool-golf.co.uk**
Terrain: **Parkland/Seaside**

Length m **5,281**	Length l **4,771**
Par/SSS m **70/67**	Par/SSS l **72/68**
Rec m **72**	Rec l **82**
Par 3 m **2**	Par 3 l **2**
Par 5 m **1**	Par 5 l **2**

Signature Hole: Second, PAR 3 from an elevated tee with river feature and village views

Captain's Hole: Ninth, PAR 4 straight forward hole with a devilish green.

Times to Avoid: Club competitions

Clubhouse: Changing rooms and toilets, bar, lounge with coffee/soup machine. Shop

Condition: Excellent (except after prolonged rain)

Memorabilia: Yes

Wildlife: Oystercatchers, herons, cormorants, gulls, ducks, salmon and trout jumping in season.

Location: To the north of village

Accommodation: Plenty of guest houses, B&Bs, and restaurants

Lost ball: 1

Comments: Each hole different, stunning scenery. Camera a must for visitors.

Fame: All incogneto

Clubs visiting: Contact Secretary

Caps visiting: Yes

C B CH T CHR CTR PG P S

65 Durness

Est: 1988

Tel: 01971 511364

Balnakeil, Durness, Sutherland, IV27 4PN
Contact: **Lucy MacKay**
Email: **lucy@durnessgolfclub.org**
Website: **www.durnessgolfclub.org**
Terrain: **Links**

Length m **5,555**	Length l **4,856**
Par/SSS m **70/67**	Par/SSS l **70/69**
Rec m **68**	Rec l **75**
Par 3 m **2**	Par 3 l **2**
Par 5 m **1**	Par 5 l **1**

Signature Hole: Ninth, short PAR 3 played across Atlantic. Not for the faint hearted.

Captain's Hole: Sixth, PAR 5 by fairway but shortened by a drive over Loch Lanlish, which fish jump and ducks swim

Times to Avoid: Sunday mornings

Clubhouse: Comfortable lounge with changing and toilet facilities. Snacks in summer.

Condition: Immaculate

Memorabilia: Ball markers, polo shirts, sweat shirts.

Wildlife: Numerous birds, rabbits, sheep, seals, porpoises, otters.

Location: 57 miles n/w of Lairg on the A838, one mile from village square.

Accommodation: MacKays rooms and restaurant.

Lost ball: 1

Comments: Offers relaxed but challenging golf in peaceful, picturesque surroundings at a reasonable price.

Fame: Peter Alliss, Ronan Rafferty, Jimmy Tarbuck

Discount: 2 for 1

Clubs visiting: Contact Secretary

Caps visiting: Negotiable

C CH T CHR CTR PG

in that a second set of tees gives the impression of playing an 18 hole course. Peter Alliss, Ronan Rafferty and Jimmy Tarbuck have all played here and have all been challenged by the signature hole, number nine, a short PAR 3 played across the Atlantic – not, then, for the faint hearted. For our money the eighth is quite the most wonderful hole, with blind shots down the machair, giving the impression of playing directly into the ocean.

Our journey now takes us east and south across Sutherland and into Caithness where we head for Lybster, on the A99, 13 miles below Wick. Enjoying wonderful views across the Moray Firth **66 Lybster** golf course is one of the shortest in the Highlands with five PAR 3s and four PAR 4s, but nonetheless provides a real test to all golfers. And accuracy is paramount for the fairways are tightly bounded by broom, brilliant in the spring, and well-tended heather, which is notoriously reluctant to release golf balls. The PAR 4 seventh and eighth play directly towards the North Sea and are a real challenge in a strong wind.

Around 40 miles south along the A9 is the inland course of **67 Helmsdale** described by the Secretary as 'an extremely pleasant challenge'. This is another short course where accuracy takes precedence over long hitting. Overlooking the famous Helmsdale salmon river, popular with Prince Charles, the Prince of Wales, the course offers views to the gold mines of Kildonan and out to sea. The fairways are fringed by bracken, gorse and broom, and present a vivid backdrop during the spring and summer. The signature fourth hole is a blind tee shot to a wide fairway while the captain's favourite is the ninth with an elevated tee to the final green.

Some 15 miles west of the famous championship course of Dornoch on the A949 is the heathland course of **68 Ardgay** at Bonar Bridge with fine views along Loch Migdale. Surrounded by sweetly scented pine trees the area is a natural home to wildlife where deer, foxes and birdlife including buzzards and osprey may

66
Lybster

Est: Unknown
Main Street, Lybster, KW1 6BL
Contact: **The Secretary**
Email: **calder4ny@btinternet.com**
Website: **www.lybstergolfclub.co.uk**
Terrain: **Heath and heather**
Length m **4,004**
Par/SSS m **62/61**
Par 3 m **5**
Par 5 m **0**
Location: **13 south of Wick on A9**

C CHR

67 Helmsdale

Est: 1895

Tel: **01431 821063**

Strath Road, Helmsdale, Sutherland, KW8 6JL
Contact: **Ronald Sutherland**
Website: **www.helmsdale.org**
Terrain: **Parkland**

Length m **3,720**	Length l **3,360**
Par/SSS m **60/60**	Par/SSS l **60/60**
Par 3 m **6**	Par 3 l **6**
Par 5 m **0**	Par 5 l **0**

Signature Hole: Fourth, blind tee shot over ridge to wide fairway

Captain's Hole: Ninth, elevated tee shot to final green

Clubhouse: Newly built clubhouse with toilets and changing rooms

Condition: Good

Memorabilia: Jumpers

Wildlife: Eagles, roe deer

Location: On the A9 approx. 40 miles north of Royal Dornoch Golf Club

Accommodation: Wide choice

Lost ball: 3

Comments: An extremely pleasant challenge

C CHR

68 Bonar Bridge – Ardgay

Est: 1904

Tel: **01863 766199**

Market Stance, Migdale Road, IV24 3EA
Contact: **John Reid**
Email: **nielsenhunter@btinternet.com**
Website: **www.bbagc.co.uk**
Terrain: **Undulating heathland**

Length m **5,162**	Length l **4,666**
Par/SSS m **68/68**	Par/SSS l **68/68**
Rec m **63**	Rec l **81**
Par 3 m **3**	Par 3 l **3**
Par 5 m **1**	Par 5 l **1**

Signature Hole: Third, PAR 3 played from an elevated tee enjoying views of loch and hills. Guarded by trees to the left and by a pond back right.

Captain's Hole: Sixth, PAR 3 with the green protected by a large pine tree and falling away on all sides.

Clubhouse: Small clubhouse with lounge and changing rooms and toilets.

Condition: Well maintained

Memorabilia: Ball markers, centenary book

Wildlife: Deer, foxes, birdlife, including buzzards and osprey.

Location: Follow A836 from Tain to Bonar Bridge. In village centre course is half a mile uphill on Migdale Road.

Accommodation: Consult Tourist Info.

Lost ball: 4

Comments: Although short the course is tree lined in parts and tight off the tee with small greens. A challenge to all abilities.

Fame: David Thomson (golf pro)

Clubs visiting: Contact Secretary

Caps visiting: Yes, Contact Secretary

C CH T CTR PG

A bad day of golf is better than a good day at work!

---

all be seen. The course is generally tight off the tee with small greens and is a challenge to all abilities. Particularly attractive is the signature third played from an elevated tee enjoying views of loch and hills and guarded by trees to the left and by a pond back right. The Captain's hole is the sixth, a PAR 3 with the green protected by a large pine tree and falling away on all sides.

At Tarbet Point, five miles south of Tain on the B9165 in Ross-shire, is the friendly, welcoming **69 Tarbat** golf course. Just a few hundred yards from the old fishing port of Portmahomack this is a rugged little course with well maintained greens making up for problems on some of the fairways. The eighth is the signature hole and requires thought and finesse while the ninth makes for a difficult final hole with out-of-bounds down the left and a narrow elevated green. There is an unlicensed tea room with an office to leave green fees. Across the Dornoch Firth there are grand views of a famous golfing coast boasting courses such as Dornoch, Golspie and Brora, not that we approve of 18 hole courses, of course! With binoculars to hand you could well see seabirds, hares, skylarks and swans

Further south in the area of Nairn is the inland **70 Cawdor Castle** course, situated on the B9090 road off the A96. The Cawdor Castle website reports that the castle was built in 1370 at a time when clubs were in constant use in Scotland, but not for sporting reasons. By comparison the golf course was something of a late comer, established in 1976 on 25 acres of mature parkland. What is the most difficult hole? The name of the second, 'No Swearing', might just give a clue.

In the area of Inverness there are two courses qualifying for inclusion in this guide, the nine-holers of Aigas, and the Loch Ness Wee Monster. The **71 Aigas** course is at the Crask of Aigas, by Beauly on the A831. Opened in 1993 and designed by Bill Mitchell PGA the course is wonderfully situated with open hill views and several holes along the Beauly

69 Tarbat

Est: 1909

Tel: **01862 871486**

Tarbatness Road, Portmahomack, Ross-shire, IV20 1XA

Contact: **Christina Ince**

Email: **golf@tarbatgolf.com**

Website: **www.tarbatgolf.com**

Terrain: **Links**

Length m **5,196**	Length l **4,839**
Par/SSS m 68/65	Par/SSS l 68/68
Rec m **64**	
Par 3 m **4**	Par 3 l **3**
Par 5 m **0**	Par 5 l **0**

Signature Hole: Eighth, requires thought and finesse, with beautiful views to the sea.

Captain's Hole: Ninth, difficult final hole with out-of-bounds down the left and a narrow elevated green.

Times to Avoid: Saturday mornings.

Clubhouse: Changing rooms and catering during the season.

Condition: Well maintained, excellent greens.

Memorabilia: Jumpers and tee shirts

Wildlife: Seabirds, hares, skylarks, swans.

Location: 6 miles from Tain on the Tarbatness Road just past the Discsovery Centre.

Accommodation: Castle Hotel, Oyster Catcher Restaurant

Lost ball: 2

Comments: A friendly welcome and good facilities, enjoyable course.

Discount: Two for One

Clubs visiting: Contact Secretary

C T CHR CTR PG

70 Cawdor Castle

Est: 1976

Tel: **01667 404401**

Cawdor Castle, Nairn, Inverness-shire, IV12 5RD
Contact: **The Secretary**
Email: **info@cawdorcastle.com**
Website: **www.cawdorcastle.com**
Terrain: **Mature parkland**

Length m **2,606**	Length l **2,606**
Par/SSS m **64/64**	Par/SSS l **64/64**
Rec m **27** (9 holes)	
Par 3 m **4**	Par 3 l **0**
Par 5 m **4**	Par 5 l **0**

Location: On B9090 south of Nairn

C B CH T CHR CTR PG P S

71 Aigas

Est: 1993

Tel: **01463 782942**

Crask of Aigas, Beauly, Inverness-shire, IV4 7AD
Contact: **The Secretary**
Email: **info@aigas-holidays.co.uk**
Website: **www.aigas-holidays.co.uk**
Terrain: **Parkland**

Length m **4,878**	Length l **4,484**
Par/SSS m **66/63**	Par/SSS l **68/65**
Par 3 m **4**	Par 3 l **4**
Par 5 m **1**	Par 5 l **2**

Location: On the A831, five miles from Beauly

C CH T CTR PG P

Aigas Golf Course

river. It is characterised by large greens and wide undulating fairways with water features, bunkers and a well-equipped practice area adjacent to the clubhouse.

If nothing else the **72 Loch Ness Wee Monster** course has one of the longest names in the world of nine-hole golf courses and a most romantic address, on Sir Walter Scott Drive. Opened in 1996 it is part of a holiday development that includes two 18 hole courses, a restaurant and conference facilities. There are generous fairways and large testing greens while the putting surfaces embrace many puzzling borrows.

Back to the ubiquitous A9 now to travel to the next course at **73 Carrbridge**, some 20 miles south of Inverness, described by the Secretary as a 'stunning and welcoming course with a challenge on every hill'. There are many natural hazards including burns, ditches and sloping fairways and all of these can be experienced on the seventh signature hole. With the mountains of the Cairngorms rising in the background a long iron shot is required to the valley floor to provide a unique and intriguing approach. Or you might prefer the first, the Captain's hole, a shortish PAR 5 which presents a difficult choice between length and accuracy – a genuine test of skill.

Set beside the River Spey just one mile south of Grantown and 15 minutes from Aviemore the 14 hole **74 Craggan** course is in the heart of Highland tourist country. There are magnificent views of the Cairngorms and the Cromdale Hills, the site of a famous battle between Government forces and Jacobites in in 1690. Amidst this glorious and romantic highland scenery the course offers two outstanding holes. The seventh is the longest on the course at 209 yards where the fairway rises 40 feet to a hilltop green while the 12th must be amongst the shortest on any course in Scotland at 51 yards. This is a great holiday course.

At Nethy Bridge on the B970 between Grantown-on-Spey and Coylumbridge a quarter of a mile north of the town is the lovely **75 Abernethy** golf course

72
Loch Ness Wee Monster

Est: 1996

Tel: **01463 713335**

Fairways, Castle Heather, Inverness, IV2 6AA
Contact: **Neil Hampton**
Email: **office@golflochness.com**
Website: **www.golflochness.com**
Terrain: **Parkland**

Length m **2,884**	Length l **2,884**
Par/SSS m **59/58**	Par/SSS l **58/58**
Par 3 m **7**	Par 3 l **7**
Par 5 m **0**	Par 5 l **0**

Clubhouse: Full facilities daily

Condition: New

Memorabilia: Yes

Wildlife: Deer, ducks

Location: Leave the A9 at Innshes/Culloden Junction and take the Sir Walter Scott Drive.

Accommodation: Travelodge on site, food at Fairways.

Comments: Short course offering challenge to golfers of all abilities

Fame: Ronan Rafferty

Clubs visiting: Contact Secretary

Caps visiting: Yes Contact Secretary

B CH T CHR SHW CTR PG D P

73 Carrbridge

Est: 1980

Tel: 08444 141415

Inverness Road, Carrbridge, Inverness-shire, PH23 3AU
Contact: **Katie Fenton**
Email: **secretary@carrbridgegolf.co.uk**
Website: **www.carrbridgegolf.co.uk**
Terrain: **Heathland**

Length m **5,402**	Length l **4,802**
Par/SSS m **71/68**	Par/SSS l **72/69**
Par 3 m **1/2**	Par 3 l **2**
Par 5 m **1**	Par 5 l **1**

Signature Hole: Seventh, distant Cairngorms rise behind the elevated green. A long iron to valley floor proides a unique and intriguing approach

Captain's Hole: First, a shortish PAR 5 which presents a difficult choice between length and accuracy – a genuine test of skill

Times to Avoid: Check with starter

Clubhouse: Small, friendly clubhouse with limited changing facilities. Full menu available during season. Small pro shop.

Condition: Excellent, full time green keeping staff.

Memorabilia: Yes

Wildlife: Abundant wildlife and impressive scenery

Location: South of Inverness, turn off the A9 at the Inverness end of the village.

Accommodation: Ample accommodation and restaurants in the area.

Lost ball: Depends on the wind

Comments: A stunning and welcoming course with a challenge on every hill.

Discount: Local Valley Discount Scheme

Clubs visiting: Discounts available for parties of ten or more

C CH T CHR CTR PG P S

74 Craggan

Est. unknown

Tel: 01479 873 283

Sionascraig, Golf Course Road, Grantown on Spey
Email: **fhglaing@btopenworld.com**
Website: **www.cragganforleisure.co.uk**
Terrain: **Inland**
Length **1,741 yards**
Par/SSS **42**

Clubhouse: The clubhouse offers good facilities and the Café is open daily from April to the end of October.

Condition: Open all year, greens cut daily during the summer

Location: Golf Course Road, Grantown on Spey

Accommodation: Tourist area with all types of accommodation and restaurants

Wildlife: Course surrounds a trout fishery. Roe deer, hares and many species of duck and other birds.

B CH T CHR SHW CTR PG D P

75 Abernethy

Est: 1893

Tel: 01479 821305

Nethy Bridge, Inverness-shire, PH25 3ED
Contact: **The Secretary**
Email: **info@abernethygolfclub.com**
Website: **www.abernethygolfclub.com**
Terrain: **Parkland**
Length m **5,052**
Par/SSS m **66/66**
Par 3 m **3**
Par 5 m **0**

Location: Quarter-of-a-mile north of Nethy Bridge on the B970

C B CH T CHR SHW CTR P

Strathtay Golf Course
Where's the 9th?

which is one of the oldest in Scotland, having been established in 1893. This is a traditional Highland course built on natural moorland and surrounded by majestic pine trees. Situated in the Cairngorms National Park Abernethy is home to many wildlife species. Red squirrels abound in the forest bordering the fairways and curlews nest between the seventh and eighth holes. Golfers may also glimpse an osprey flying over the course back to its home at the famous Loch Garten centre – the ancestral home of the osprey in Scotland.

Visitors are warmly welcomed at **76 Fort Augustus** golf course which is situated one mile south of the historic town on the A82. The course is bounded on one side by Scots Pines lining the back of the Caledonian Canal and on the other by the heather and gorse-clad Glengarry Mountains. This is another nine-holer with two sets of tees to each hole, giving outward and inward halves of different length and aspect, with pars of three, four and five over each nine holes. Clubs and trolleys can be hired and there is a lounge bar for relaxing after the game.

The parkland and woodland course of **77 Spean Bridge** hides behind the eponymously named railway station and hotel on the gentle slopes below Ben Nevis some eight miles north of Fort William. The clubhouse has a rustic charm and few facilities although trolleys are available when there are club members in attendance. It is in remarkably good condition for a course with no permanent green keepers and attended only by dedicated unpaid members. The signature sixth hole is a 323 yard PAR 4 demanding a long carry over rough and bog before an approach to a fast flat green. The seventh, the Captain's favourite, also involves a long carry from the tee, but it is the eighth which offers the most problems. Described by one member as a 'rascal of a hole' it is undoubtedly the most difficult on the course with the trees to the right of the fairway appearing to draw the ball magnetically.

76
Fort Augustus

Est: 1924

Tel: **01320 366660**

Market hill, Fort Augustus, Inverness-shire, PH32 4AU

Contact: **The Secretary**

Email: **fortaugustusgc@aol.com**

Website:
   www.fortaugustusgc.webeden.co.uk

Terrain: **Heathland**

Length m **5,379**

Par/SSS m **67/67**

Par 3 m **4**

Par 5 m **2**

Location: One mile south of Fort Augustus on A82

C B CH T SHW

77
Spean Bridge

Est: 1950's

Tel: **07710 105478**

Station Road, Spean Bridge, Highlands,
PH34 4EU
Contact: **The Secretary**
Email: **kenneth.dalziel@openreach.co.uk**
Website: **www.speangolf.org**
Terrain: **Parkland**

Length m **4,542**	Length l **3,768**
Par/SSS m **68/63**	Par/SSS l **68/62**
Par 3 m **2**	Par 3 l **2**
Par 5 m **0**	Par 5 l **0**

Signature Hole: Sixth, long carry over rough
and bog on fairway.

Captain's Hole: Seventh, another long carry to
the fairway.

Clubhouse: Tiny, with honesty box

Condition: Very good for a course with no
permanent greens staff.

Wildlife: Varied

Location: Turn right at the Spean Bridge Hotel
in the centre of the village when travelling
north.

Accommodation: Spean Bridge Hotel

Lost ball: 3

Comments: Very friendly with lovely views.
Watch out for the eighth 'A rascal of a hole'.

Clubs visiting: Contact Secretary

Caps visiting: Contact Secretary

C CH

Tarbat Golf Course

HEARTLANDS

Perthshire, Angus, Dundee and Fife

78
Saline

Est: 1912

Tel: **01383 852591**

Kinneddar Hill, Saline, Fife, KY12 9LT
Contact: **Adrienne Lyon**
Email: **salinegolfclub@btconnect.com**
Website: **www.salinegolfclub.org**
Terrain: **Hilly Parkland**

Length m **5,302**	Length l **4,840**
Par/SSS m **66/66**	Par/SSS l **68/68**
Rec m **62**	Rec l **73**
Par 3 m **2**	Par 3 l **2**
Par 5 m **0**	Par 5 l **0**

Signature Hole: Eighth, difficult PAR 3, well bunkered with a small green

Captain's Hole: Sixth, panoramic view from tee, long downhill fairway to bunkered green.

Times to Avoid: Monday and Thursday evenings and Saturdays

Clubhouse: Comfortable but rather basic, occasional catering

Condition: Excellent

Memorabilia: Sweaters, tee shirts and hats

Wildlife: Pheasants, crows, buzzards, horses, hares, hedgehogs

Location: Leave M90 at Junction four at Kelty, take the B913 and follow signs for Dollar. Clubhouse at top of hill into village.

Accommodation: Saline Hotel or Kirklands House, Saline

Lost ball: 1

Comments: A beautiful course in very good condition offering an enjoyable challenge with many stupendous views.

Clubs visiting: Contact Secretary
Caps visiting: Contact Secretary

C B CH T CHR CTR PG

The Heartlands of Scotland is the spiritual home of golf, embracing the oldest and most famous golf courses in the world. In this area are to be found the holy grail of golf, courses such as the Old Course at St Andrews, Carnoustie, Gleneagles, Blairgowrie, Lundin Links and the wonderful Taymouth Castle at Kenmore. Golfers flock here from all over the world to experience the thrill of walking the same turf as Old Tom Morris, course designer supreme and four times Open winner.

For our purposes, however, we are going to forget all these crown jewels of world golf and concentrate instead on our target courses, the rich heritage of finely cut hidden gem nine-holers which inhabit the Heartlands of Scotland.

The greatest concentration of our courses are in Fife, which in view of its noble history is entirely appropriate, followed by an equally generous scattering in Perthshire and then a couple, which should certainly not be ignored, in the northern area of Angus.

As most visitors arriving to the heartlands will approach from the Forth Road Bridge we will start the tour in Fife working from the most westerly course of Saline across to the most easterly at St Andrews. **78 Saline** golf course is sited at Kinneddar Hill, Saline and approached from junction four on the M90 north of the Forth Road Bridge. Laid out over a south-facing hillside the course has tremendous views over the Forth Bridges, the hills of the Lothian's and Ochil Hills. Test yourself on the signature eighth, a difficult PAR 3 which is well bunkered with a small green. Or you might prefer the sixth and its panoramic view from the tee and a drive downhill to a bunkered green. There is a practice area, nets and putting green.

All the remaining courses in Fife are to the east of

Lairds Golf Course, Guthrie Castle

the M90 motorway. The first on our list is **79 Lochore Meadows** at Crosshills, Lochgelly, a relatively long inland course set in rolling parkland with superb views across Loch Ore. At 6,414 yards the par is 72 and SSS 71. A wide range of facilities is available at the clubhouse.

Close by is **80 Auchterderran** an interesting course set in quiet and peaceful surroundings in the former mining village of Cardenden. Opened in 1904 the inland layout demands a thoughtful approach to the game while the clubhouse offers trolley hire, showers and restaurant facilities.

Not far away and a mile north of Kirkcaldy is **81 The Cluny** a challenging course with a wide variety of holes. It undulates gently with the roll of the land and has fairways running in all directions with the River Ore alongside the second and the eighth. The river also crosses the fairway of the signature hole, the third, a 152 yard PAR 3. The tees are mostly large and the greens in good condition. If the family are not all into golf then there is a great range of other activities on offer. They could try their hand at archery or even clay pigeon shooting – and if all else fails treat them to a golf lesson at the driving range.

Some seven miles east of junction five on the M90 is the **82 Leslie** golf course at Balsillie Laws, between Glenrothes and Loch Leven. It is a tricky, parkland course with a burn offering a hazard on a number

79
Lochore Meadows

Est: Unknown
Tel: **01592 414345**
Lochore Meadows Country Park, Crosshill, Lochgelly, Fife, KY5 8BA
Contact: **The Secretary**
Website: **www.fifegolftrust.co.uk**
Terrain: **Parkland**
Length m **6,414**
Par/SSS m **72/71**
Par 3 m **2**
Par 5 m **2**
Location: From M90 turn off at Junction 4 for Holbeath

C B CHR SHW CTR PG P

Tarbert Loch Fynne Golf Course

80 Auchterderran

Est: 1904
Tel: **01592 721579**
Woodend Road, Cardenden, Fife, KY5 0NH
Contact: **The Secretary**
Website: **www.fifegolftrust.co.uk**
Terrain: **Parkland**
Length m **5,122**
Par/SSS m **72/72**
Par 3 m **3**
Par 5 m **0**
Location: In the village of Cardenden, six miles north of Kirkcaldy

C B BG CH T CHR SHW
CTR PG D P S

81 The Cluny

Est: 2002
Tel: **01592 720374**
Cluny, By Kirkcaldy, Fife, KY2 6QU
Contact: **Operations Manager**
Email: **enquiries@clunygolf.co.uk**
Website: **www.clunygolf.co.uk**
Terrain: **Parkland, mildly undulating**
Length m **4,624**   Length l **4,570**
Par/SSS m **64/64**   Par/SSS l **64/64**
Par 3 m **4**   Par 3 l **4**
Par 5 m **0**   Par 5 l **0**
Signature Hole: Third, PAR 3 over river
Location: One mile north of Kirkcaldy on B922

C B CH T CHR CTR PG
D P

82 Leslie

Est: Unknown
Tel: **01592 620040**
Balsillie Laws, Leslie, Glenrothes, Fife, KY6 3EZ
Contact: **The Secretary**
Email: **secretarylgc@hotmail.co.uk**
Website: **www.lesliegolfclub.com**
Terrain: **Parkland**
Length m **4,940**
Par/SSS m **62/65**
Par 3 m **5**
Par 5 m **0**
Location: Seven miles east of Junction five, M90

C B CHR

Lochcarron Golf Course

of holes. With five PAR 3's and the rest PAR 4's the course plays over 4,940 yards and a has par of 62.

What do Henry Cooper, Jimmy Tarbuck and Jim Leishman all have in common, apart from a love of golf? They have all played **83 Bishopshire** golf course a lovely hillside heathland course at Kinnesswood, three miles east of Kinross on the A911. Laid out in 1903 on the foothills of Bishopshire there are panoramic views over Loch Leven and Kinross. The signature fourth offers a downhill tee shot with trouble on left and right and with a blind second to the green. The war memorial at the entrance to the course is particularly moving.

84 Milnathort is a parkland course in the centre of the village, a mile north of Kinross. Fairly long for a nine-holer it plays over 5,985 yards with a par of 71 (sss 69). Have any famous people played here? 'Who knows', says the secretary, 'they all wear masks'. Must all be golfing bandits! This is a typical inland course with lush fairways and excellent greens. Strategically placed copses of trees demand accurate tee shots while variety is provided by the addition of different tees and greens for certain holes. The signature fourth is surrounded by bunkers, fronted by hawthorn trees and a dry ditch in front of the green. For non-golfers Loch Leven National Nature Reserve close by is brimming with wildlife and history.

North of Glenrothes on the A912 is **85 Falkland** golf course, an inland course playing over 4,988 yards. This is a short but tough test of golf set deep in a lush farmland area known as the 'Howe of Fife'. Established in 1975, gentle hills provide a backdrop, but as the website pictures show the course is subject to flooding. Heroically, this is described as simply 'a new water hazard'.

Although men are welcome to play at **86 Lundin Ladies** these days they play solely as guests. All the members are women and they fill all the responsible positions at the club, which is certainly unique in Britain and possibly in the world, although we stand

83 Bishopshire

Est: 1903

Tel: **01592 780203**

Kinnesswood, Perthshire, Kinross, KY13 7HX
Contact: **Toni Cascarino**
Website: **www.bishopshiregolfclub.com**
Terrain: **Hillside course on the foothills of Bishopshire. Panoramic views over Loch Leven and Kinross.**

Length m **4,571**

Par/SSS m **66/63**	Par/SSS l **63/63**
Rec m **62**	
Par 3 m **3**	Par 3 l **3**
Par 5 m **0**	Par 5 l **0**

Signature Hole: Fourth, down hill 430m trouble on left and right, blind second shot to green.

Captain's Hole: Same as Signature

Times to Avoid: Saturday 1–2pm

Clubhouse: Changing facilities, no lockers or showers. Catering on request.

Condition: Average 6/10

Memorabilia: Possibly on request

Wildlife: Deer, rabbits, birds and GLIDERS!

Location: North on M90, follow signs for Glenrothes, then one mile past Scottish Gliding Centre.

Accommodation: Lomond View Hotel, Kinnesswood.

Lost ball: 2

Comments: At £8 a round it is well worth the effort. Outstanding views from the top of the course.

Fame: Henry Cooper, Davy Sword, Jimmy Tarbuck, Jim Leishman.

Clubs visiting: Phone ahead to arrange

C CHR CTR PG D P

84 Milnathort

Est: 1910

Tel: **01577 864069**

South Street, Milnathort, Kinross, KY13 9XA
Contact: **Ken Dziennik**
Email: **milnathort.gc@btconnect.com**
Website: **www.milnathortgolfclub.co.uk**
Terrain: **Undulating parkland**

Length m **5,985**	Length l **5,405**
Par/SSS m **71/69**	Par/SSS l **72/71**
Rec m **61**	
Par 3 m **2**	Par 3 l **2**
Par 5 m **3**	Par 5 l **4**

Signature Hole: Fourth, surrounded by bunkers fronted by hawthorn trees and a dry ditch in front of green

Times to Avoid: Evenings and Saturdays.

Clubhouse: Full facilities with a friendly bar in a lovely setting.

Condition: Excellent

Memorabilia: Yes

Wildlife: Loch Leen National Nature Reserve close by brimming with wildlife and history.

Location: One mile north of Kinross. M90 Junction six (north) or Junction seven (south)

Accommodation: Thistle Hotel, Royal Hotel, Jolly Beggars

Lost ball: 1

Comments: Undulating inland course with lush fairways and excellent greens. Strategically placed copses of trees require accurate tee shots. Variety is provided by the addition of different tees and greens for certain holes.

Fame: Who knows – they all wear masks!

Discount: Perthshire nine-hole tickets.

Clubs visiting: Contact Secretary

C B T CHR SHW CTR PG D P

85 Falkland

Est: 1975

Tel: **01337 857404**

The Myre, Falkland, Fife, KY15 7AA
Contact: **The Secretary**
Email: **falklandgolfclub@gmail.com**
Website: **www.falklandgolfclub.com**
Terrain: **Undulating parkland**

Length m **4,988**	
Par/SSS m **68/65**	
Par 3 m **3**	
Par 5 m **1**	

Location: Nine miles from the M90 motorway

C CH CHR

86 Lundin Ladies

Est: 1891

Tel: **01333 320832**

Woodielea Road, Lundin Links, Fife, KY8 6AR
Contact: **Liz Davidson**
Email: **llgolfclub@tiscali.co.uk**
Website: **www.lundinladiesgolfclub.co.uk**
Terrain: **Parkland**

Length l **4,730**	
Par/SSS l **68/68**	
Par 3 m **2**	
Par 5 m **0**	

Signature Hole: Second, 262 yards with standing stones on the fairway

Times to Avoid: Wednesdays

Clubhouse: Ladies only. Tea and coffee available. Men welcome to play course.

Condition: Excellent

Wildlife: Pheasants, ducks

Location: Follow A915 signposted St Andrews, turn left opposite bank in village.

Accommodation: Three local hotels within walking distance.

Lost ball: 2

Fame: John McTeer

C T CHR

Elie Golf Course

ready to be corrected on this point. Established in 1891 and designed by James Braid the course is close by the famous Lundin course. It is an inland layout playing over 4,730 yards to a PAR/SSS of 68. Enjoy the signature second, a 262 yard PAR 4 where shots that strike the amazing standing stones on the fairway are seldom rewarded with a friendly rebound. Set on Lundin Links the course is to the west of the village off the A915.

Further along the coast on the A917 are the soft undulating fairways of the **87 Elie Sports Club**. The nine hole-course is a delight to play with superb views overlooking the Firth of Forth. The links turf and generous greens are in excellent condition all year round. This course was opened in 1899 and was originally known as The Ladies Course, which seems to have been something of a habit in this part of the world. The Pavilion café offers good catering year round and there is a well stocked golf shop and internet access. The signature hole is the ninth, a short downhill PAR 3 with the Firth of Forth as a backdrop. The tricky 103 yard sixth is the Captain's favourite.

Stretched along the Fife shoreline between Pittenweem and Anstruther, and just nine miles from St Andrews, is the **88 Anstruther** course, founded in 1890. It has seen many changes during its long history from a seven hole course, with trenches through the middle and poles scattered over the greens to stop gliders landing during the war, to its present nine-hole status. All of the holes have names relating to its history with the 'Magazine' so called because one of the huts beside the hole was used during the war to store ammunition magazines. George Murray, the 2004 Scottish Amateur Champion is the current record holder. Watch for the signature fifth, 235 yards with gorse banking on the right and out-of-bounds on the left and played from an elevated tee. The Captain's favourite is the next hole played from an elevated tee where the wind can have a major influence.

87
Elie Sports Club

Est: 1899

Tel: **01333 330955**

Golf Course Lane, Elie, Fife, KY9 1AS
Contact: **Ian Muir (Professional)**
Email: **eliesportsclub@btconnect.com**
Website: **www.eliesportsclub.co.uk**
Terrain: **Parkland**

Length m **4,160**	Length l **4,160**
Par/SSS m **64/64**	Par/SSS l **64**
Par 3 m **4**	Par 3 l **4**
Par 5 m **0**	Par 5 l **0**

Signature Hole: Ninth, short downhill PAR 3 with Firth of Forth as backdrop.

Captain's Hole: Short Sixth, 103 yards very tricky

Times to Avoid: Very busy July and August

Clubhouse: Pavilion café catering year round, Golf shop and internet access

Condition: Very good all year round

Memorabilia: Yes

Wildlife: Pheasant, partridge, hares

Location: From Elie to Earlsferry turn right up Golf Club Lane adjacent to Golf House Club

Accommodation: Eat at Pavilion

Lost ball: 1

Comments: Perfect for beginners young and OAP's

Fame: Bill Campbell (1964 US amateur and Walker Cup Captain) Sir Michael Bonnallack, Ronnie Shade, Peter Thomson (Five times Open Champ, Honorary Member.)

Clubs visiting: Contact Professional or
Caps visiting: Secretary

C B CH T CHR CTR PG D P S

Est: 1890

Tel: **01333 310956**

Marsfield, Shore Road, Anstruther, Fife, KY10 3DZ

Contact: **Steven Gardner**

Email: **secretary@anstruthergolf.co.uk**

Website: **www.anstruthergolf.co.uk**

Terrain: **Seaside links**

Length m **4,498**	Length l **4,128**
Par/SSS m **62/63**	Par/SSS l **66/66**
Rec m **60**	
Par 3 m **5**	Par 3 l **3**
Par 5 m **0**	Par 5 l **0**

Signature Hole: Fifth, 235 yds with gorse banking on right and out-of-bounds on left – played from elevated tee.

Captain's Hole: Sixth, 150 yds played from an elevated tee

Times to Avoid: Saturdays

Clubhouse: Locker rooms, male and female showers in gents locker room. Bar, Dining room, catering in summer season.

Condition: Generally good

Memorabilia: Ball markers, pitch repairers, ties.

Wildlife: Seabirds, occasionally dolphins and porpoises

Location: On entering Anstruther follow signs downhill from Craws Nest Hotel.

Accommodation: Craws Nest Hotel, choice of restaurants

Lost ball: 3

Comments: Friendly club with some beautiful views of the Firth of Forth. Fifth is one of the hardest PAR 3's ever.

Fame: George Murray 2004 Scottish Amateur Champion and course record holder.

Discount: Bunkered

Clubs visiting: Contact Secretary

Caps visiting: Free golf for gentlemen

C B T CHR SHW CTR PG

Killin Golf Course

The next stop on this part of the tour is the **89 St Andrews Balgove** links course. Millions of words have been written about the world famous courses of the 'Auld Grey Toon' but very few about this fine little nine-holer. The golfing authorities at the town describe this as an authentic golfing experience for children, beginners and families and it enjoys all the facilities of the Eden Clubhouse with dining, locker rooms, showers and information. In other words a perfect family holiday course.

Does the idea of dressing up in clothes that were the height of fashion in the 1920s and trying your hand with a hickory mashie-niblick appeal? If so head for Cupar and the new **90 Kingarrock Hickory Golf** centre, situated on the Hill of Tarvit just outside the town. Kingarrock is an exciting concept organised by the National Trust for Scotland with the help of Trust members and a number of enthusiastic golfers. It is on the site of an older course which was ploughed up in the 1930s as part of the war effort, and was re-opened for the first time in over 70 years on 28 June 2008. In keeping with its early history it may only be played with hickory, or wooden, shafted clubs.

The novel idea put together by the Trust means that all players will be provided with original hickory clubs, such as a spoon, driving iron, mashie, niblick and putter, and an original canvas and leather bag, together with softer golf balls and tees that represent the early 20th century golfing experience.

In addition to all this the green fee includes a nip of whisky or port to get into the spirit of the 'roaring twenties', the guarantee of half-an-hour gap between parties on the first tee, 'Da Anderson' ginger beer and shortbread on completion of the round, and a miniature of Kingarrock malt whisky in a quality gift bag. Also free entry to the Hill of Tarvit Mansion House. Visitors who bring their own hickory clubs may play for half price.

This is a terrific idea from an organisation usually

89 St Andrews Balgove

Est: 1972

Tel: 01334 466666

Balgove Golf Course, St Andrews Links Trust, St Andrews, Fife, KY16 9SF
Contact: **The Secretary**
Email: **reservations@standrews.org.uk**
Website: **www.standrews.org.uk**
Terrain: **Links**

Length m **3,040**	Length l **3,040**
Par/SSS m **60/60**	Par/SSS l **60/60**
Par 3 m **6**	Par 3 l **6**
Par 5 m **0**	Par 5 l **0**

Clubhouse: Eden Clubhouse, offers dining, locker room, showers and information

Condition: Excellent

Memorabilia: Yes

Wildlife: Coastal and grassland wildlife

Location: Signposted off the A91

Accommodation: Swilcan Restaurant and the Links Clubhouse

Comments: An authentic golfing experience for children, beginners and families.

Clubs visiting: Contact reservations@standrews.org.uk

C B BG CH CHR SHW CTR PG D P S

C Clubhouse **B** Bar **BG** Buggy **CH** Club Hire **T** Trolley **CHR** Changing Rooms **SHW** Showers

90
Kingarrock Hickory Golf

Re-opened: 2008

Tel: **01334 653421**

Golf & Thistle, Forrester's Cottage, Hill of Tarvit,
Cupar, Fife, KY15 5PB
Contact: **Michelle Thissen**
Email: **michelle@kingarrock.com**
Website: **www.kingarrock.com**
Terrain: **Parkland**
Length m **4,044**
Par/SSS m **68/68**
Par 3 m **3**
Par 5 m **1**

Clubhouse: Yes

Condition: Improving

Memorabilia: Yes

Location: From Cupar take the A914 past the
railway station and turn left onto the A916
as soon as you leave the town heading
south. Follow the road for a mile to the top
of the hill. The Mansion House and Golf
Course are signposted to the left.

Comments: A highly unusual golfing
experience

Fame: Peter Alliss, Phil Tufnell

Greenkeeper/President
Falkland Golf Course

C

Kingarroch House

thought of as somewhat stuffy and we recommend all keen nine-holers to flock to Kingarrock.

Our final destination on the Fife tour is **91 Cupar Hilltarvit** golf course just off the A91 St Andrews to Milnathort road, and situated on the Ceres Road near the cemetery. Founded on the 7 November 1855 this is believed to be the oldest nine-hole course in the world and provides a tricky challenge and entertainment to players of all abilities. Lee Trevino and Eric Thomson have played here and no doubt enjoyed the signature eighth, a dog-leg requiring an accurate drive and a good second to a small green cut into the side of a hill. The Captain's hole is the sixth, an uphill PAR 3 to a large green commanding superb views.

Travelling east the first course in the Perthshire sector is a nine-holer at another world famous golfing destination, Gleneagles, where they have thoughtfully provided the **92 Gleneagles Wee** course. Played over just 2,962 yards and with a par of 27, every hole on this genuinely 'wee' course is a PAR 3. The course is worth playing just for the imaginative names given to the holes, such as 'Fairy Hillocks', 'Cheery Lea', 'Kelpie's Howff', 'Fickle Fortune' and 'Clean Drap'.

One of the most popular courses in the Perthshire area is at **93 Dunning** on the A934 just a few miles off the A9. This is a short but challenging parkland course with a series of stone-built bridges crossing a burn that comes into play on a number of holes. There are also trees and well-placed bunkers adding to the entertainment. Snacks are available in the clubhouse which is due for upgrading. The tight driving first hole, 'The Avenue', is the signature hole with mature trees on both sides to a slightly sloping and well-guarded green. 'Craig Rossie', the eighth, is the Captain's favourite with an inviting tee shot to a generous fairway, but then a tough up-hill second into the prevailing wind to a wickedly sloping green.

Three miles south of Crieff at the entrance to the village on the A822 is the parkland **94 Muthil** Golf

---

91
Cupar Hilltarvit

Est: 1855

Tel: **01334 653549**

Hilltarvit, Cupar, Fife, KY15 5JJ
Contact: **John M. Houston**
Email: **cupargc@fsmail.net**
Website: **www.cupargolfclub.co.uk**
Terrain: **Hillside parkland**

Length m **5,153**	Length l **4,612**
Par/SSS m **68/68**	Par/SSS l **68/68**
Rec m **61**	
Par 3 m **2**	Par 3 l **2**
Par 5 m **0**	Par 5 l **0**

Signature Hole: Eighth, dog-leg requiring acccurate drive and good second to small green cut into side of hill.

Captain's Hole: Sixth, uphill PAR 3 to large green commanding superb views.

Times to Avoid: Wednesday evenings. Saturday mornings

Clubhouse: Small, comfortable and friendly, bar with snacks/lunches

Condition: Tidy with fast greens

Memorabilia: Ball markers, jumpers, hats, glass ware

Location: On Ceres Rd off A91 in Cupar, near cemetery.

Accommodation: Eden House Hotel, Clubhouse bar

Comments: Possibly oldest nine-hole course in UK – tricky course with superb views.

Fame: Lee Trevino, Eric Thomson

Discount: 2 for 1

Clubs visiting: Discounts available for parties

C B CH T CHR SHW CTR PG

92
Gleneagles PGA Nat. Ac.

Est: Unknown

Tel: **01764 662231**

Gleneagles, Auchterarder, Perthshire, PH3 1NF
Contact: **The Secretary**
Email: **resort.sales@gleneagles.com**
Website: **www.gleneagles.com**
Terrain: **Heathland**
Length m **2,962**
Par/SSS m **54/54**
Par 3 m **9**
Par 5 m **0**

Location: Turn north off A9 at A823 – halfway
between Perth and Sterling

**C B BG CH T CHR SHW
CTR PG D P S**

93
Dunning

Est: 1907

Tel: **01764 684747**

Rollo Park, Station Road, Dunning, Perthshire,
PH2 0QX
Contact: **D. Cantlay**
Email: **secretary@dunninggolfclub.co.uk**
Website: **www.dunninggolfclub.co.uk**
Terrain: **Parkland**

Length m **4,894**		Length l **4,506**
Par/SSS m **66/64**		Par/SSS l **66/66**
Rec m **62**		
Par 3 m **3**		Par 3 l **3**
Par 5 m **0**		Par 5 l **0**

Signature Hole: First, 270 yards tight driving
hole through mature trees onto a protected
green

Captain's Hole: Eighth, 350 yards with a tough
up-hill approach shot into the prevailing
wind to a wickedly sloping green

Times to Avoid: Saturday mornings,
Wednesday afternoons

Clubhouse: All facilities and some catering

Condition: Excellent

Memorabilia: Yes

Wildlife: Nothing special

Location: Signposted from Dunning village

Accommodation: The Dunning Inn and the
Kirkstyle Inn

Lost ball: 2

Comments: Welcoming friendly club, modestly
priced and a short but challenging course.
Good greens with water hazards.

Clubs visiting: Contact Secretary

**C CH T CHR SHW CTR PG
P**

94
Muthil

Est: 1912

Tel: **01764 681523**

Peat Road, Muthill, Perthshire, PH5 2AD
Contact: **The Secretary**
Email: **muthillgolfclub@btconnect.com**
Website: **www.muthillgolf.co.uk**
Terrain: **Parkland**

Length m **4,673**	Length l **4,525**
Par/SSS m **66/63**	Par/SSS l **66/67**
Par 3 m **3**	Par 3 l **3**
Par 5 m **0**	Par 5 l **0**

Location: At entrance to Muthill village on
A822, three miles south of Crieff

C CH T CHR CTR PG

Family Golf.
Oatridge Golf Course

Course. 'Our aim', says the website, 'is to be the friendliest golf club in the world'. Established in 1912 and re-opened in 1935 by Jessie Anderson, later Jessie Valentine the three times British Ladies Amateur Champion, this undulating course has narrow fairways, small well-bunkered greens and picturesque views of Strathearn and the Grampians.

At **95 Crieff** the Dornock Course was originally part of the main course and retains many of the original Simpson/Braid features. In its earlier incarnation as an 18 hole course it hosted the Scottish Professional Championship in 1963. Today it is a delightfully tricky nine-holer in rolling parkland on the Perth Road just outside the town. The first is the signature hole and offers a difficult choice whether to flirt with the o.o.b. down the right which offers the best approach shot to the green or to play safely to the centre of the fairway. The Captain prefers the short PAR 3 eighth played to an elevated green with a water hazard short and left of the putting area.

To the west on the A85 is the **96 Comrie** golf course, enjoying a hilly parkland setting where imaginative use of natural gradients has created some interesting holes. When we played there the captain was also the greenkeeper and the condition of the course is a testament to his hard work. As usual for rural Perthshsire the scenery is gorgeous. A monument to a long dead lord features in the views from the modern clubhouse. 'Happy Valley', the fifth, is the signature hole a PAR 3 over a valley from an elevated tee to an elevated green. The downhill PAR 4 seventh plays around a copse of trees and is the Captain's favourite.

Further along the road and across the River Earn is the equally delightful course of **97 St Fillans**, situated on the South Loch Earn Road. This parkland course is surrounded by hills and mountains with abundant wildlife including roe deer, pheasants, wild goats and capercaillies. The course was laid out in 1903 to a design by Willie Auchterlonie, professional at St Andrews and one time Open Champion. The

95
Crieff – Dornock

Est: 1891

Tel: **01764 652909**

Crieff Dornock Course, Perth Road, Crieff, Perthshire, PH7 3LR
Contact: **Mr David Murchie**
Email: **bookings@crieffgolf.co.uk**
Website: **www.crieffgolf.co.uk**
Terrain: **Undulating parkland**

Length m **4,540**	Length l **4,052**
Par/SSS m **64/63**	Par/SSS l **64/64**
Par 3 m **4**	Par 3 l **4**
Par 5 m **0**	Par 5 l **0**

Signature Hole: First, Out-of-bounds to the right, but farther right the better for easier second shot.

Captain's Hole: Eighth, short PAR 3, elevated green, water hazard short and left of green.

Clubhouse: Full clubhouse and catering facilities.

Condition: Very good

Memorabilia: Yes

Wildlife: Normal Perthshire flora and fauna

Location: On main A85 at the eastern entrance to Crieff

Accommodation: Contact TIC 01764 652578

Comments: The Dornock was originally part of the main course and as such retains many of the original Simpson/Braid features.

Fame: In its 18 hole format it hosted the Scottish Pro Championship in 1963.

Discount: Perthshire Highland Ticket.

Clubs visiting: Must book in advance.

Caps visiting: Courtesy for Club Secretaries

C B BG CH T CHR CTR PG D P S

96
Comrie

Est: 1891

Tel: **01764 670055**

Laggan Braes, Comrie, Perthshire, PH6 2LR
Contact: **The Secretary**
Email: **comriegolf@tiscali.co.uk**
Website: **www.comriegolf.co.uk**
Terrain: **Parkland**

Length m **6,040**	Length l **5,250**
Par/SSS m **70/70**	Par/SSS l **74/72**
Par 3 m **2**	Par 3 l **2**
Par 5 m **1**	Par 5 l **3**

Signature Hole: Fifth, elevated tee to an elevated green over fierce rough.

Captain's Hole: Seventh, downhill dog-leg around a copse of trees

Times to Avoid: Mondays and Tuesdays

Clubhouse: Modern. Limited catering

Condition: Excellent

Memorabilia: Yes

Wildlife: Deer and birds

Location: On A85 between Lochearnhead and Perth

Lost ball: 5

Comments: Fairly long for a nine-hole course with a number of demanding holes. Gorgeous scenery.

Discount: 2 for 1 if staying in Comrie

Clubs visiting: Contact Secretary

Caps visiting: Contact Secretary

C CH T CHR SHW CTR PG P

97
St Fillans

Est: 1903

Tel: **01764 685312**

South Lochearn Road, St Fillans, Perthshire, PH6 2NJ
Contact: **The Secretary**
Email: **stfillansgolf@aol.com**
Website: **www.st-fillans-golf.com**
Terrain: **Parkland**

Length m **6,054**	Length l **5,412**
Par/SSS m **69/69**	Par/SSS l **74/72**
Par 3 m **2**	Par 3 l **1**
Par 5 m **1**	Par 5 l **2**

Signature Hole: Third, elevated tee to a short PAR 4 with wonderful mountain views.

Captain's Hole: Fifth, dog-leg to the right around a prominent rock to an elevated green.

Times to Avoid: Saturdays in summer

Clubhouse: Yes

Condition: Very good

Memorabilia: Yes

Wildlife: Roe deer, pheasants, wild goats, capercaillie

Location: Close to River Earn and Loch Earn, 12 miles west of Crieff on A85

Accommodation: Achray House

Lost ball: 5

Comments: Beautifully situated course laid out in 1903 to a design by golf icon Willie Auchterlonie, professional at St Andrews and Open Champion.

Discount: Contact Secretary

Clubs visiting: Contact Secretary

C BG CH T CHR CTR

signature hole is the third, a short PAR 4 played from an elevated tee with distracting mountain views. But the Captain prefers the fifth, a right angled dog-leg around a prominent rock to an elevated green.

A little to the north on the country road to Dunkeld and five miles north of Crieff is the **98 Foulford Inn** course, a PAR 3 heathland layout and one of the highest courses in Scotland with stunning views of the Perthshire hills. In fine condition, and with good greens, the course drains well and normally can be played year round, weather and wind permitting. Enjoy the signature fourth a short PAR 3 played to a peninsular green in the middle of a pond which is stocked with trout. You are not, however, invited to bring your fishing rod.

All the remaining Perthshire courses in the Heartlands are further north and the next three are all in the beautiful Tay Valley. The **99 Strathtay** course is loved by everyone who has been fortunate enough to play it, the views from the sixth and eighth tees are worth the green fee alone. Halfway between Ballinluig on the A9 and Aberfeldy on the A827 the course was established in 1909 on wooded parkland and there is a challenge on every hole. The second features a relatively new elevated green played as a dog-leg from right to left. The next hole is immediately behind an island of tall oak trees and requires a skillfull shot over the trees or played as a dog-leg, again from right to left. The brilliant fifth, Spion Kop, is the signature hole played up a steep hill to a hidden green in a hollow over the summit. A wonderful hole on a course which encapsulates everything that could be hoped for of a Highland nine-holer.

At the eastern end of Loch Tay, on the opposite bank of the River Tay to the championship length Taymouth Castle course, is the relatively new **100 Mains of Taymouth** golf course, blessed with wonderful scenery and providing a good golfing test. It was built in 1992 at the Mains of Taymouth on pleasantly undulating parkland and it measures 6,052 yards from the medal tees and 5,502 yards from the yellows. Watch

98 Foulford Inn

Est: 1995

Tel: **01764 652407**

Sma' Glen, Crieff, Perthshire, PH7 3LN
Contact: **Mr Brian Beaumont**
Email: **foulford@btconnect.com**
Website: **www.foulfordinn.co.uk**
Terrain: **Parkland with water hazards**
Length m **1,832**
Par/SSS m **54/54**
Rec m **24 (9 holes)**
Par 3 m **9**
Par 5 m **0**

Signature Hole: Fourth, peninsular green in the middle of a pond

Captain's Hole: Fourth.

Clubhouse: Foulford Inn, adjacent.

Condition: Drains well, good greens.

Wildlife: Moorland birds, hares, roe deer and raptors.

Location: Five miles north of Crieff on the A822 direction Dunkeld.

Accommodation: At adjacent Hotel.

Lost ball: 1

Comments: One of the highest courses in Scotland, stunning views.

Clubs visiting: Negotiable

C B CH CTR PG

99 Strathtay

Est: 1909

Tel: **01887 840373**

Strathtay, By Pitlochry, Perthshire, PH9 0PG
Contact: **Mr Alistair Robinson**
Email: **strathtay@aol.com**
Website: **www.strathtaygolfclub.com**
Terrain: **Hilly with some beautiful views.**
Length m **3,774**   Length l **2,943m**
Par/SSS m **62/61**   Par/SSS l **62/61**
Par 3 m **5**   Par 3 l **5**
Par 5 m **0**   Par 5 l **0**

Signature Hole: Fifth, Spion Kop 218 yard PAR 4. Up a steepish slope with hidden green in a hollow over the summit.

Captain's Hole: Same as signature

Times to Avoid: Sunday 12.30 – 2pm.

Clubhouse: Unattended, honesty box checked by greenkeeper, changing facilities and toilets.

Condition: Greenkeeper lavishes care on it and is very proud of it.

Memorabilia: Ball markers, jumpers and hats.

Wildlife: All forms of animal and bird life.

Location: Follow signs on main Ballinluig to Aberfeldy road.

Comments: An unusual course incorporating unique holes and beautiful views.

Discount: Perth and Kinross Tickets

C T CHR

100 The Mains of Taymouth

Est: 1992

Tel: **01887 830226**

Mains of Taymouth, Kenmore, Perthshire, PH15 2HN
Contact: **Golf Manager**
Email: **info@taymouth.co.uk**
Website: **www.taymouth.co.uk**
Terrain: **Undulating parkland**
Length m **6,052**   Length l **5,064**
Par/SSS m **70/69**   Par/SSS l **70/71**
Rec m **64**   Rec l **72**
Par 3 m **3**   Par 3 l **3**
Par 5 m **2**   Par 5 l **2**

Signature Hole: Second, tee off from a wooded outcrop to an elevated green requiring accuracy and courage.

Captain's Hole: Fourth, almost 600 yards PAR 5 with huge beech trees.

Clubhouse: Modern and comfortable with good facilities.

Condition: First class.

Memorabilia: Small selection

Wildlife: Pheasant, deer and much more.

Location: Across River Tay from Kenmore.

Accommodation: Kenmore Hotel, Mains of Taymouth Cottages and The Courtyard.

Lost ball: 8

Comments: Lovely scenery and good test of golf

Fame: Many!

Discount: Two for One

Clubs visiting: Contact Secretary

C B BG CH T CHR SHW CTR PG P S

Foulford Inn Golf Course

out for the second, which tees off from a wooded out-crop to an elevated green requiring accuracy and courage. The long hitting Captain prefers the 600 yard PAR 5 fourth which is lined with huge beech trees.

Travelling now to the western end of Loch Tay is **101 Killin** golf course just outside the town on the road above the loch. The course, designed by Stirling golf professional John Duncan, was established in 1911 by a dedicated group of farmers, tradesmen, merchants and professional people. They chose a glorious setting for the course lying at the start of beautiful Glen Lochay with its river sweeping past the first fairway to end in Loch Tay. Money for the club-house which dates from 1922 was partially raised by a concert given by the Covent Garden Opera Company in the village. There are four PAR 3's, four PAR 4's and a PAR 5 ninth which has been described as the most scenic closing hole in Scotland.

On the B8079 north of Pitlochry lies the **102 Blair Atholl** parkland golf course in the heart of beautiful countryside. A river runs by three of the holes on

101
Killin

Est: 1911

Tel: **01567 820312**

Killin, Perthshire, FK21 8TX
Contact: **The Secretary**
Email: **info@killingolfclub.co.uk**
Website: **www.killingolfclub.co.uk**
Terrain: **Undulating parkland**

Length m **5,036**	Length l **4491**
Par/SSS m **66/65**	Par/SSS l **66/67**
Par 3 m **4**	Par 3 l **4**
Par 5 m **1**	Par 5 l **1**

Location: West end of Loch Tay

C B BG CH T CHR SHW
CTR PG P S

Killin Clubhouse and buggies

C Clubhouse B Bar BG Buggy CH Club Hire T Trolley CHR Changing Rooms SHW Showers

102
Blair Atholl

Est: Unknown

Tel: **01796 481407**

Invertilt Road, Blair Atholl, Perthshire, PH18 5TG
Contact: **The Secretary**
Email: **info@blairathollgolf.co.uk**
Website: **www.blairathollgolfclub.co.uk**
Terrain: **Parkland**
Length m **5,816**
Par/SSS m **70/68**
Par 3 m **2**
Par 5 m **1**

Location: At the end of the road after turning
left at the Tilt Hotel

C B CH T CHR SHW CTR

Notice at Killin Golf Club

Mains of Taymouth

this inland course creating an attractive natural hazard on a relatively long nine-holer, with a yardage of 5,816 and a PAR/SSS of 70/68.

Blairgowrie is our next port of call, home to some of Scotland's finest Championship courses. We are not concerned with the famous courses of Lansdowne and Rosemount, but with the lesser known **103 Blairgowrie Wee** golf course. This heathland layout plays through heather-lined avenues of pine and silver birch and stretches 4,704 yards with a PAR/SSS of 64/63; there are four PAR 3's and five PAR 4's. The Wee Course formed part of the original layout designed by Dr Alistair McKenzie of Augusta National and Cypress Point fame.

Some 14 miles from Blairgowrie the **104 Piperdam** PAR 3 nine-holer is part of a major holiday complex complete with an 18 hole course, 72 self catering holiday lodges, gym, swimming pool and steam room, and a 40 acre fishing loch. It is host to Scotland's National Par 3 Championship each September. The holes range from 211 yards to 111 yards and demand the use of every club in the bag. The signature hole is the interesting second at 155 yards which has an elevated tee, bright yellow flowering gorse in front of the green and mature oak trees on the banks of a burn that surrounds the other three sides of the green.

At Alyth, close by the A926, is the **105 Strathmore Leitfie Links** golf course, which despite its name is a parkland course. This is a complete golfing centre with an 18 hole course, a ten bay covered driving range and a golf academy, as well as a modern clubhouse offering all facilities and lovely views along the Vale of Strathmore. The Leitfie course requires accurate play with PAR 3s ranging in length from 83 yards to 212 yards and small greens.

Tom Lehman and Ken Brown have both played the **106 Dalmunzie** course at the Spittal of Glenshee, just off the Blairgowrie to Braemar road. There are spectacular views on this parkland course in a wild setting where red deer, birds of prey, oystercatchers,

103
Blairgowrie Wee

Est: Unknown

Tel: **01250 872622**

Rosemount, Blairgowrie, Perthshire, PH10 6LG
Contact: **The Secretary**
Email: **office@theblairgowriegolfclub.co.uk**
Website: **www.theblairgowriegolfclub.co.uk**
Terrain: **Heathland**
Length m **4,704**
Par/SSS m **64/63**
Par 3 m **4**
Par 5 m **0**
Location: 15 miles north east of Perth off A93

C B BG CH T CHR SHW
CTR PG P S

Bonnybridge Golf Course

104
Piperdam

Est: 2009

Tel: **01382 585012**

Piperdam Golf and Leisure Resort, Fowlis,
Dundee, DD2 5LP
Contact: **Owen Leslie**
Email: **proshop@piperdam.com**
Website: **www.piperdam.com**
Terrain: **Parkland**

Length m **2,798**	Length l **2,420**
Par/SSS **27/27**	
Course Record: **25**	
Par 3s **9**	
Par 5s **9**	

Signature Hole: 155 yard 2nd played from an elevated tee to a well protected green.

Clubhouse: Lounge bar and full restaurant. Gym and swimming pool. 72 self-catering holiday lodges, hot tubs and saunas.

Condition: USGA spec greens provide perfect putting surfaces all year.

Location: Six miles from Dundee on the Coupar Angus road.

Lost ball rating: 1 or 2

Secretary's Comments: Great fun. Great for occasional golfers and juniors as it is not too taxing but will also provide a real test for experienced golfers.

C B CH T CHR SHW CTR
PG D P S

105
Strathmore Leitfie Links

Est: 1996

Tel: **01828 633322**

Strathmore Golf Centre, Leroch, Alyth,
Perthshire, PH11 8NZ
Contact: **The Secretary**
Email: **enquiries@strathmoregolf.com**
Website: **www.strathmoregolf.com**
Terrain: **Parkland**

Length m **3,332**	Length l **3,332**
Par/SSS m **58/58**	Par/SSS l **58**
Par 3 m **7**	Par 3 l **7**
Par 5 m **0**	Par 5 l **0**

Clubhouse: Bar

Condition: Good

Location: A926 Blairgowrie to Kirriemuir road, south of Blackbird Inn.

Comments: The friendly place to play golf.

Clubs visiting: Contact Secretary

Caps visiting: Contact Secretary

C B BG CH T CHR SHW
CTR PG D P S

106
Dalmunzie

Est: 1920

Tel: **01250 885226**

Spittal of Glenshee, Blairgowrie, Perthshire,
PH10 7QE
Contact: **Simon Winton**
Email: **enquiries@dalmunziecottages.com**
Website: **www.dalmunziecottages.com**
Terrain: **Hilly upland**

Length m **4,198**	Length l **3,710**
Par/SSS m **60/60**	Par/SSS l **66/66**
Par 3 m **6**	Par 3 l **5**
Par 5 m **0**	Par 5 l **2**

Clubhouse: Dalmunzie House Hotel acts as clubhouse and starter. Turreted baronial country house set on 6500 acre sporting estate.

Condition: Good

Wildlife: Red deer, birds of prey, oystercatchers, curlew, lapwings

Location: 18 miles north of Blairgowrie and 15 miles south of Braemar on A93 at the Spital of Glenshee.

Accommodation: Dalmunzie House

Lost ball: 4

Comments: Fantastic views, spectacular shots to be played on a course originally designed by Alistair MacKenzie.

Fame: Tom Lehman, Ken Brown

Clubs visiting: Terms on application

C B CH CTR

curlew and lapwings can often be seen. Originally designed by Alistair Mackenzie, this is another course which claims to be amongst the highest in Britain, which put simply means that the wind is always going to be a significant factor. Nearly every hole on this challenging course brings its own difficulties and rewards, and is a wonderful way to walk the heather, play some sport and enjoy the views for a couple of hours.

The tour now takes us across into the small county of Angus where the **107 Lairds Course**, at the magnificent Guthrie Castle on the A932 from Forfar, is the result of one man's vision and desire to create for himself one of the best 'target' courses in Scotland. The course was laid out in 1994/95 and in 2003 it was opened to the public by reservation only. For the higher handicap player it is a daunting course where anything less than the correct club selection and an accurate tee shot is severely punished. Amongst the celebrities to play this little gem are Stuart Wilson, Open Champion, Gary Hay, Ryder Cup player, and Hamish McAlpine, the Scottish goal-keeper. At Guthrie Castle they claim that every hole is 'signature', but select the ninth with its downhill tee shot across a loch to a small crowned green protected by loch and burn, and the fourth, 145

107
Guthrie Castle – Lairds Course

Est: 1998

Tel: **01241 828691**

Guthrie Castle, Guthrie, Friockheim, Angus, DD8 2TP
Contact: **Paul Morris**
Terrain: **Parkland with loch**

Length m **5,514**	Length l **4,818**
Par/SSS m **68/70**	Par/SSS l **70/70**
Rec m **34 (9 holes)**	
Par 3 m **3**	Par 3 l **3**
Par 5 m **1**	Par 5 l **1**

Signature Hole: Ninth, downhill across loch to small crowned green protected by loch and burn.

Captain's Hole: Fourth, 145 yards across loch to elevated green with steep bank to rear.

Clubhouse: New clubhouse with bar and changing rooms.

Condition: Excellent

Memorabilia: Yes

Wildlife: Hawks, swans, deer, red squirrels

Location: Guthrie Castle, centre of Angus

Accommodation: 5 Gables Guest House, Arbroath, Gordons Restaurant and B & B

Lost ball: 7

Fame: Stuart Wilson (open champion), Gary Hay,(Ryder Cup player) Hamish McAlpine (Scottish goalkeeper)

Discount: Carnoustie Country

C B BG CH T CHR SHW

Did you know ?

The average number of ball marks made on greens per round is 8 per golfer. Assuming only 130 rounds are played each day on your course, your greens receive 1,040 impressions daily, 31,000 per month or more than 374,000 per year. Are you wondering how to make a putt under these conditions ?
REPAIR YOUR PITCHMARKS

Thorntrees Ltd.

Cupar Hilltarvit Clubhouse

yards across the loch to an elevated green with a steep bank to the rear as being typically terrifying.

Close to the world famous 'Open' course of Carnoustie is the new **108 Kingennie** layout, which surrounds the Forbes of Kingennie Estate. Although not particularly long it has been described as a 'risk and reward' course where any golfer prepared to avoid the 'safe' shot will score well. There are fine amenities at Kingennie including a driving range with target golf and an 18 hole putting green built to USGA standards. From Dundee follow the A92 for Arbroath, then leave at West Grange roundabout and follow signs for Forbes of Kingennie.

Midway between Dundee and Aberdeen in the village of Edzell is the final course to feature in the Heartlands tour. Situated at the gateway to the Grampians and in the foothills of the Angus Glens the **109 West Water** course is the latest addition to the Edzell golf complex where the main course was first laid out in 1895. This is an inland tree-lined course with the River West Water proving the principal hazard. Visitors are advised to beware the ninth signature hole, a short but heavily-bunkered challenge with the River providing a beautiful backdrop. The Captain says he prefers the second, a PAR 5 which demands an accurate second shot to avoid trees on either side. On a good day the non-golfers can spot pheasant, deer and buzzards.

108
Kingennie

Est: 2007

Tel: **01382 350777**

Kingennie, Broughty Ferry, Dundee, DD5 3RD
Contact: **The Secretary**
Email: **info@forbesofkingennie.com**
Website: **www.forbesofkingennie.com**
Terrain: **Inland**
Length m **5,600**   Length l **5,600**
Par/SSS m **68/68**
Rec m **68/68**

C B BG CH T CHR SHW CTR PG P S

109
Edzell – West Water

Est: 2001

Tel: **01356 648291**

Dunlappie Road, Edzell, Angus, DD9 7TF
Contact: **Ian Farquhar**
Email: **secretary@adzellgolfclub.net**
Website: **www.edzellgolfclub.com**
Terrain: **Parkland**

Length m **4,114**	Length l **3,580**
Par/SSS m **64/60**	Par/SSS l **64/62**
Par 3 m **5**	Par 3 l **5**
Par 5 m **1**	Par 5 l **1**

Signature Hole: Ninth, heavily bunkered short hole with River West Water providing a beautiful backdrop.

Captain's Hole: Second, PAR 5 which demands accurate second shot to avoid trees on either side.

Clubhouse: Refurbished clubhouse with full catering facilities available.

Condition: Excellent

Memorabilia: Ball markers, hats, jumpers

Wildlife: Pheasants, deer, buzzards

Location: When entering Edzell from south turn left at tweed shop, continue half a mile – course on left.

Comments: Tree lined course with West Water proving a hazzard.

Caps visiting: Contact Secretary

**C B BG CH T CHR SHW
CTR PG D S**

St Medan Golf Course

NORTH EAST
Aberdeen and Grampian

Twenty-one of Scotland's beautiful nine-hole golf courses lie in the North East, a rugged area of mountains and heathland and hardy North Sea fishermen. The area is famous for wonderful malt whiskies from its many distilleries, for historical castles, such as Balmoral a favourite with the Royal family for decades, and for game fishing on the great rivers of the Don, the Dee and the Spey which cut through the area.

For us it is another rich playground of wonderful golf courses waiting to be discovered. Many are in the south-eastern corner around the area of Aberdeen and this tour starts with these before moving north along the coast from Aberdeen and then finishing in the north west corner at Cove Sea and Kinloss, taking in a couple of inland courses on the way.

On the B9119 some five miles north of Aboyne, **110 Tarland** is a tricky parkland course with beautiful views across the Dee Valley. Two of the most popular holes are the fourth and fifth. The 385 yard, PAR 4 fourth crosses a burn to a tight green surrounded by pine trees and on the fifth, a long PAR 3, there are more trees challenging the wayward tee shot.

Set in spectacular scenery, on a south facing site beside Loch of Aboyne the **111 Aboyne Loch Tiger** golf course claims to offer the challenges of championship golf on a compact nine-hole layout. The course is at Formaston Park to the east side of the village above the A93. The signature hole ninth is played from an elevated tee over the loch to a two-tier green where two bunkers guard the direct approach. An equally demanding hole is the eighth, the captain's favourite. A 435 yard PAR 4, the tee faces downhill with magnificent views to east, south, and west to the Cairngorms National Park. A narrow green makes for a difficult second shot. While there watch out for abundant wildlife which can include, ospreys,

110
Tarland

Est: 1908

Tel: **01339 881000**

Aberdeen Road, Tarland, Aboyne, Aberdeenshire, AB34 4TB

Contact: **The Secretary**

Email: **secretary@tarlandgolfclub.co.uk**

Website: **www.tarlandgolfclub.co.uk**

Terrain: **Parkland**

Length m **5,816**

Par/SSS m **66/68**

Par 3 m **3**

Par 5 m **0**

Location: Follow A974 from Aberdeen in village of Tarland

C B T CHR CTR PG P

C Clubhouse B Bar BG Buggy CH Club Hire T Trolley CHR Changing Rooms SHW Showers

111
Aboyne Loch Tiger

Est: 2002

Tel: **013398 86444**

Tiger, Aboyne, Aberdeenshire, AB34 5BR
Contact: **Derek McCulloch**
Email: **info@thelodgeontheloch.com**
Website: **www.thelodgeontheloch.com**
Terrain: **Parkland**

Length m **5,200**	Length l **4,700**
Par/SSS m **68/65**	Par/SSS l **70/68**
Par 3 m **4**	Par 3 l **4**
Par 5 m **2**	Par 5 l **3**

Signature Hole: Ninth, played from an elevated tee over the loch to a two tier green. Two bunkers guard the direct approach. The hole is also in full view of the Lodge to add to the pressure.

Captain's Hole: Eighth, a 435 yard PAR 4. The tee faces downhill with magnificent view East, South and West to the Cairngorms National Park. A narrow green makes for a difficult second shot.

Clubhouse: Excellent, more like a private Country Club at Play and Pay prices. Restaurant seats 120, Function Room, 75. Glass fronted deck for 100.

Condition: Good

Wildlife: Ospreys, buzzards, sparrowhawks, kestrels, lapwing, oystercatchers, woodpeckers, cuckoos, coots, and rare butterflies.

Location: One mile east of Aboyne signposted. 'The Lodge'.

Accommodation: Local B & B/ eat at the Lodge

Lost ball: 3

Comments: Tee times always available on one of the most scenic and challenging courses in the NE.

Clubs visiting: Contact for terms

C B BG CH T CHR SHW CTR PG

Lumphanan Golf Course

buzzards, sparrowhawks, kestrels, lapwings, oyster-catchers, coots and rare butterflies. As Bertie Wooster once said, 'I couldn't concentrate on my golf for the uproar of the butterflies in the adjoining meadow'.

A more recent addition to the facilities at the Aboyne Loch Golf Centre is the **112 Pussycat** course, following a customer demand for a driving range and an easier nine-hole course. The signature hole remains the ninth, while the Captain's favourite is the downhill PAR 5 sixth, where a well-sited bunker makes it difficult to reach the green in two strokes.

Not far away make time for a visit to **113 Lumphanan** a small village in rural Deeside set in the heart of Macbeth country. It was here that Macbeth died at the hands of Malcolm in 1057 and for a time he was buried in the local graveyard. The Lumphanan course was originally established, a little later, in 1924 but fell into disrepair in the 1960's until rescued by local enthusiasts in the 1990's. With the help of Lottery funding it finally re-opened for play again in the spring of 2001 boasting six new greens, 15 new tees and ten new bunkers. The heathland course measures 3,718 yards over 18 holes with a PAR/SSS of 61. Members have great respect for the PAR 3 fifth where the fairway slopes away to the left with two bunkers guarding the small elevated green.

In the same area of Royal Deeside is another heathland course at **114 Torphins**, a hilly course with outstanding views of the Grampians. Features on this course are the blind shots from a number of tees. The condition of the course is good and the greens are recognised as excellent. Beware of distractions from pheasants and deer – although they have been known to move courteously to the edge of the fairway to permit uninterrupted play. The PAR 4 sixth is a 'notorious' hole with a 90 degree dog-leg left and a tight fairway with heather and o.o.b. problems to negotiate while the narrow green, with some deceptive borrows, falls away at the back.

The Paul Lawrie Golf Centre situated two miles from

112
Aboyne Loch – Pussycat

Est: 2006

Tel: **013398 86444**

Aboyne, Aberdeenshire, AB34 5BR
Contact: **Derek McCulloch**
Email: **info@thelodgeontheloch.com**
Website: **www.thelodgeontheloch.com**
Terrain: **Parkland**
Length m **3,600**
Par/SSS m **62**

C B T CHR CTR PG P

113
Lumphanan

Est: 1924

Tel: **01339 883480**

Main Road, Lumphanan, Banchory, AB31 4PX
Contact: **The Secretary**
Email: **info@lumphanangolfclub.com**
Website: **www.lumphanangolfclub.co.uk**
Terrain: **Heathland**

Length m **3,718**	Length l **3,372**
Par/SSS m **62/61**	Par/SSS l **64/61**
Par 3 m **5**	Par 3 l **4**
Par 5 m **0**	

Location: South side of main road from Torphins

C B CHR SHW CTR

114
Torphins

Est: 1895

Tel: **01339 882115**

Bog Road, Torphins, Aberdeenshire, AB31 4JU
Contact: **S. W. MacGregor**
Email: **stuartmacgregor5@btinternet.com**
Website: **www.torphinsgolfclub.co.uk**
Terrain: **Parkland**

Length m **4,777**	Length l **4,577**
Par/SSS m **64/64**	Par/SSS l **66/69**
Rec m **59**	
Par 3 m **4**	Par 3 l **4**
Par 5 m **0**	Par 5 l **1**

Times to Avoid: Alternate Saturdays and Sundays

Clubhouse: Comfortable with good facilities. Catering at weekends

Condition: Excellent

Memorabilia: Ball markes, tees

Wildlife: Pheasants and deer

Location: One mile from village towards Lumphanan, signposted

Accommodation: Learney Arms Hotel, Torphins

Lost ball: 3

Comments: Scenic with wonderful views, in good condition and a good test of golf.

Discount: Bunkered

Clubs visiting: Discounts for groups

Caps visiting: Free if notified in advance

C T CHR SHW CTR PG

Lybster Golf Course

the Brig'o'Dee was opened in 2005 and in addition to the **115 Paul Lawrie** PAR 3 course embraces a 26 bay floodlit driving range, fully equipped teaching studios, putting green and bar/ restaurant. Since opening it has attracted some big golfing names such as Open Champion Paul Lawrie, and Harry Bannerman, a member of the 1971 Ryder Cup team. Dormie one-up in the USA going down the last against the great Arnold Palmer, Harry had to settle for a halved match after an outrageous birdie three from Arnie. The 140 yard third is the signature hole with a carry over water to an 'L' shaped undulating green. The secretary also recommends the eighth which demands a long iron shot again over water to a small green.

The sad news at the beginning of 2013 is that the **116 Inchmarlow** complex, Banchory has gone into administration and for the moment the fine nine-holer has been closed. We understand that buyers are being sought and it is possible that it may open again at some point. There is a danger that when nine-holers are part of a major holiday complex they can be brought down by problems elsewhere in the organisation. The nine-hole course was opened in 1997 and although no hole is longer than 350 yards there are formidable hazards including burns, ponds and dykes which guard many of the greens. Two of the more outstanding holes are the fifth, a PAR 3, played from a tree lined tee over a pond to an undulating green, and the eighth which is a dog-leg left with the tee shot played through a narrow gap in trees over a dyke with a ditch lurking to cause more trouble.

The furthest south of this group of courses is **117 Auchenblae** which is ten miles south west of Stonehaven and three miles off the A90. This is a well maintained course with excellent greens set in beautiful scenery. Beware of the second with its split level green guarded by four pot bunkers. Wildlife here includes buzzards, skylarks and the ubiquitous rabbit.

Great advantages of having nine-hole courses as part of a bigger complex are the additional facilities

115
Paul Lawrie Golf Centre

Est: 2005

Tel: 01224 865750

Paul Lawrie Golf Centre, South Deeside Road, Aberdeen, AB12 5YN
Contact: **Garry Russell**
Email: **shop@paullawriegolfcentre.co.uk**
Website: **www.paullawriegolfcentre.co.uk**
Terrain: **Parkland**

Length m **2,672**	Length l **2,182**
Par/SSS m **54/54**	Par/SSS l **54/54**
Par 3 m **9**	Par 3 l **9**
Par 5 m **0**	Par 5 l **0**

Signature Hole: Third, 140 yard carry over water to a 'L' shaped green undulating green.

Captain's Hole: Eighth, long iron carry over water to a small green.

Clubhouse: Good facilities with changing rooms, showers and catering

Condition: First Class

Memorabilia: Yes

Wildlife: Swans, ducks, deer and eagles.

Location: Signposts to Ardoe House Hotel on South Deeside Road.

Accommodation: Ardoe House Hotel, Aspire Restaurant

Lost ball: 5

Comments: A fair yet challenging course. You will be impressed.

Fame: Paul Lawrie, Harry Bannerman, Scot Henderson.

C B T CHR SHW CTR PG D P S

116
Inchmarlow Queens

Est: 1997

Tel: 01330 826422

Glassel Road, Banchory, AB31 4BQ
Contact: **Andrew Shinie**
Email: **secretary@inchmarlo.com**
Website: **www.inchmarlow.com**
Terrain: **Undulating parkland in mature pine forest**

Length m **4,300**	Length l **3,602**
Par/SSS m **64/62**	Par/SSS l **66/61**
Par 3 m **4**	Par 3 l **3**
Par 5 m **0**	Par 5 l **0**

Signature Hole: Fifth, PAR 3 from tree lined tee over pond to undulating green

Captain's Hole: Eighth, dog-leg left – tee shot played though a narrow gap in trees over dyke with ditch lurking.

Clubhouse: Small, modern with all facilities

Condition: Excellent

Memorabilia: Yes

Wildlife: Buzzards, deer and red squirrels

Location: One mile west of Banchory on A93 to Aboyne on Torphins road.

Accommodation: Raemoir House Hotel

Lost ball: 1

Comments: A beautiful short but scenic course which tests all facets of your game.

Fame: Paul Lawrie, Ronan Rafferty, cast of Emmerdale

Clubs visiting: By arrangement

Caps visiting: Prior arrangement

C B BG CH T CHR SHW CTR PG D P S

117
Auchenblae

Est: 1890

Tel: 01561 320002

'Per Linwood', Auchenblae, Aberdeenshire, AB30 1TX
Contact: **Jenny Thomson**
Website: **www.auchenblaegolfcourse.co.uk**
Terrain: **Parkland**

Length m **4,434**
Par/SSS m **64/61**
Par 3 m **4**
Par 5 m **0**

Captain's Hole: Second, split level green guarded by four pot bunkers.

Times to Avoid: Wednesday evenings

Clubhouse: Though unpretentious it has changing facilities and serves light refreshments.

Condition: Good with excellent greens

Wildlife: Buzzards, skylarks, rabbits

Location: 25 miles south of Aberdeen and three miles west of the A90 between Stonehaven and Laurencekirk

Accommodation: Ramsey Arms Hotel, Fettercairn

Comments: Well maintained course with excellent greens, beautiful scenery

Clubs visiting: By arrangement

C T CHR CTR

Larkhall Golf Course

available. This is true at **118 Deeside, Blairs** golf course where there is a modern clubhouse with locker room, bar, restaurant, snooker and pro shop. This is an inland course by the River Dee and laid out over a parkland terrain. The original nine-hole course was opened in 1903 but later extended to 18 holes. The balance was restored in 1984 when the Blairs course was opened, playing over 5,042 yards with PAR/SSS of 68.

The nine-hole course at **119 Hazlehead**, just to the west of the Aberdeen city centre between the N. Deeside Road and Lang Stracht, is also part of a golfing complex embracing in addition two 18 hole courses plus a pitch and putt. The nine-hole course has wide fairways and a marked absence of rough, making it the perfect starting point for the enthusiastic beginner. The best known hole on this course is the 'Sahara', a rare desert with grass, which is a massive 502 yards PAR 5.

The next stage of this tour of the North East takes us above Aberdeen with five coastal courses and one inland. At the Bridge of Don, five miles north of Aberdeen, is the **120 Murcar Links** golf club which has the unusual claim to fame that it once owned its own railway company to transport players from Aberdeen to the course. The 18 hole course opened in June 1909 on a wild stretch of coast and the James Braid designed Strabathie nine-hole course opened some 30 years later. This course has more of an inland nature than the links style of the main course, and each hole has two separate tees making for an interesting and demanding test for all abilities of golfer.

Towards Peterhead and some 27 miles from Aberdeen on the A975 off the A90 is **121 Cruden Bay St Olafs** golf course, part of the Cruden Bay Golf Club, home club of Paul Lawrie the Open Champion, where it is said that golf was first played as early as 1791. The development of golf on this site was prompted by the extension north of the railway, whose owners built a grand hotel and the golf course. Both declined during the depression of the 30's and the

118
Deeside, Blairs

Est: 1903

Tel: **01224 869457**

Golf Road, Bieldside, Aberdeen, Grampian, AB15 9DL
Contact: **The Secretary**
Email: **admin@deesidegolfclub.com**
Website: **www.deesidegolfclub.com**
Terrain: **Parkland**
Length m **5,042**
Par/SSS m **70/67**
Par 3 m **4**
Par 5 m **2**
Location: Six miles west of Aberdeen city centre off A93

C CH T CHR SHW CTR PG P S

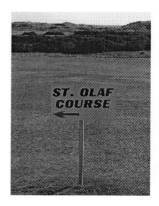

ST. OLAF COURSE

119
Hazlehead

Est: Unknown

Tel: 01224 326293

Hazlehead Park, Aberdeen, AB15 8BD
Contact: **The Secretary**
Email: **information@sportaberdeen.co.uk**
Website: **www.sportaberdeen.co.uk**
Terrain: **Parkland**
Length m **5,540**
Par/SSS m **70/70**
Par 3 m **2**
Par 5 m **1**
Location: Four miles west of Aberdeen city
centre

C B CH T CTR PG P S

120
Murcar Links

Est: 1940s

Tel: 01224 704354

Bridge of Don, Aberdeen, AB23 8BD
Contact: **The Secretary**
Email: **golf@murcarlinks.com**
Website: **www.murcarlinks.com**
Terrain: **Links**
Length m **5,369**
Par/SSS m **70/67**
Par 3 m **1**
Par 5 m **0**
Location: Five miles north of Aberdeen city
centre off A90

C B CH T CHR SHW CTR
PG D P S

121
Cruden Bay St Olafs

Est: 1960s

Tel: 01779 812285

Aulton Road, Cruden Bay, Peterhead, AB42 0NN
Contact: **Rosemary Pittendrigh**
Email: **elaine@crudenbaygolfclub.co.uk**
Website: **www.crudenbaygolfclub.co.uk**
Terrain: **Links**
Length m **4,926**   Length l **4,692**
Par/SSS m **64/64**   Par/SSS l **66/68**
Par 3 m **4**   Par 3 l **4**
Par 5 m **0**   Par 5 l **1**
Times to Avoid: Tuesdays and Saturday
mornings
Clubhouse: Modern clubhouse with full bar
and catering
Condition: Excellent
Memorabilia: Yes
Location: 25 miles north of Aberdeen and nine
miles south of Peterhead on A90
Accommodation: Red House Hotel,
Kilmarnoch Arms Hotel, St Olaf Hotel.
Comments: Interesting and testing
Caps visiting: Free golf for gentlemen and
ladies

B T CHR SHW CTR PG D P
S

St Fillans Golf Course.
First Tee

hotel was eventually razed in the 1950s. Fortunately golf has survived and the course at St Olaf's is a links layout with wonderful views. Played over 4,926 yards the PAR/SSS is 64, this course boasts some of the best holes on a nine-holer anywhere in the world. The PAR 4 346 yard fourth is an outstanding hole. There is a slight dog-leg to the left with fairway and green, surrounded by gorse and whins. Be warned, a shot through the green here is a goner.

In that home of some of the hardiest fishermen in Britain is the **122 Peterhead** Old Golf Course and the nine-hole New Golf Course. Bounded by the North Sea at Craigiewan and the River Ugie to the south and west, the courses have a traditional links style with the nine holer built around the practice area. Enjoying all the facilities of a big club the New Course plays to 4,394 yards and a PAR/SSS of 62.

Moving inland to rural Aberdeenshire some 28 miles from Aberdeen on the A947 is the relatively new **123 Fyvie** golf course, opened in 2005, and situated on a hilltop just south of the village with views of Fyvie Castle and Bennachie. The course is well suited to high handicappers as there are no long carries over water or deep rough. A three tier green is a feature of the tree-lined signature PAR 3 sixth, while the Captain's choice is the 475 yard PAR 5 seventh. This offers a double dog-leg and a green protected by two ponds, not to mention a rather haughty Llama whose main pleasure in life is said to be collecting lost golf balls.

122
Peterhead

Est: 1892

Tel: **01779 472149**

Craigewan Links, Peterhead, Aberdeenshire, AB42 1LT
Contact: **The Secretary**
Email: **enquiries@peterheadgolfclub.co.uk**
Website: **www.peterheadgolfclub.co.uk**
Terrain: **Links**
Length m **4,474**
Par/SSS m **62/62**
Par 3 m **5**
Par 5 m **0**
Location: Off Golf Road at north end of town

C B BG CH T CHR SHW CTR PG D P S

Comrie Clubhouse

123
Fyvie

Est: 2004

Tel: 01651 891166

Fyvie, Turriff, Aberdeenshire, AB53 8QR
Contact: **Mr Alexander Rankin**
Email: **info@fyviegolfcourse.co.uk**
Website: **www.fyviegolfcourse.co.uk**
Terrain: **Hill course, links style fairways**

Length m **2,738**	Length l **2,424**
Par/SSS m **67**	Par/SSS l **67**
Rec m **67**	
Par 3 m **2**	Par 3 l **2**
Par 5 m **1**	Par 5 l **1**

Signature Hole: Sixth, PAR 3 with three tier green.

Captain's Hole: Seventh, PAR 5, double dog-leg, water feature beside green

Clubhouse: Bar, restaurant. Changing rooms, shower facilities in Gents changing room. Licence from 7am–1am.

Condition: Well manicured, fast draining.

Memorabilia: Balls, markers, pitch mark repairers, jumpers.

Wildlife: Osprey, marlin, kestrel and curlew

Location: From South on A947, turn off right before village, then one mile up this road.

Accommodation: Eat at clubhouse.

Lost ball: 1

Comments: Stunning views, friendly and course well presented.

Fame: John Black.

Clubs visiting: Discount for 16–20 persons on full day package.

C B BG CH T CHR SHW CTR

Fyvie Golf Club

Back to the coast at Fraserburgh we come to the world's oldest golf course with its original name. Fraserburgh is also the seventh oldest golf club in the world so it has a long and distinguished history. The nine-hole **124 Rosehill** course is a more recent addition to the club and unlike the main James Braid designed links Corbie 18 hole course, is a parkland style course played over 4,832 yards to a PAR/SSS of 66/63.

A little further along the coast is the **125 Rosehearty** course on open dunes beside the beach on the outskirts of this little Royal Burgh. The course is a mixture of parkland and links and has a rugged beauty with lovely views across the Moray Firth. Like many coastal courses the turf is lush and forgiving while the greens are small and testing. Playing over 4,154 yards with a PAR/SSS of 62 the Captain's favourite hole is the fourth, played from a blind tee and with a dog-leg to the green.

The final four courses in the North East area are some 40 miles to the west. Around ten miles south of Elgin on the A941 is **126 Rothes** an inland course set well back from the town where a claim to fame is that it was once played by Radio 2's Terry Wogan. Opened in 1990 and located in the Spey Valley, on the famous Whisky Trail, the parkland course features lush tree-lined fairways. The Captain's preferred hole is the PAR 3 fourth with a pot bunker at the front of the green, trees to the left and a water hazard to the rear. The signature hole is the PAR 3 sixth played over a gulley to a long narrow green.

As the name suggests **127 Covesea Links** golf course is on the coast at Duffus, a short drive from Lossiemouth and not much more than a three wood from Gordonstoun Public School, with its long history of Royal patronage. Unusually it is a 12 hole links course and qualifies for inclusion here by the simple fact that it is not an 18 holer. The course has been closed for a couple of years, but we understand there are plans to re-open soon. The natural dunes and testing greens mixed with the sea breeze provide a

124 Rosehill

Est: 2002

Tel: **01346 516616**

Philorth Links, Fraserburgh, Aberdeenshire, AB43 8TL
Contact: **Mr George M Young**
Email: **secretary@fraserburghgolfclub.org**
Website: **www.fraserburghgolfclub.org**
Terrain: **Flat links**

Length m **4,832**	Length l **4,572**
Par/SSS m **66/63**	Par/SSS l **70/63**
Par 3 m 3	Par 3 l 3
Par 5 m 0	Par 5 l 2

Clubhouse: New clubhouse, 2006. Male, female and visitors locker rooms also showers. Fully licensed and catering available.

Condition: Very good all year especially summer months.

Memorabilia: In due course

Wildlife: Game birds, rabbits etc

Location: Turn right at first roundabout on entrance to Fraserburgh and follow signs

Accommodation: Tufted Duck Hotel, Findlay's, Heathhill. All within ten minutes of Course.

Lost ball: 2

Comments: Flat. Nice and relaxing. First tee and ninth green adjacent to clubhouse.

Clubs visiting: Discounts available

Caps visiting: Negotiable

C B CH T CHR SHW CTR P P S

C Clubhouse **B** Bar **BG** Buggy **CH** Club Hire **T** Trolley **CHR** Changing Rooms **SHW** Showers

125
Rosehearty

Est: 1873

Tel: **01346 571250**

C/o Masons Arms Hotel, Rosehearty,
Fraserburgh, AB43 7JJ
Contact: **Scott Hornal**
Email: **roseheartygc@yahoo.com**
Terrain: **Links**
Length m **4,154**
Par/SSS m **62/62**

Rec m **60**	Rec l **74**
Par 3 m **5**	Par 3 l **5**
Par 5 m **0**	Par 5 l **0**

Captain's Hole: Fourth, blind tee shot and dog-leg to green.

Clubhouse: Changing rooms only

Condition: Very good.

Memorabilia: Yes

Wildlife: Yes

Location: Three and a half miles west of Fraserburgh on the coast road

Accommodation: Masons Arms Hotel.

Lost ball: 5

Comments: A testing course for any golfer.

Fame: Hamish Love

Clubs visiting: Yes

Caps visiting: Yes

C CH T CHR CTR PG P

126
Rothes

Est: 1990

Tel: **01340 831676**

Blackhall, Rothes, Aberlour, Aberdeenshire,
AB38 7AN
Contact: **Kenneth MacPhee**
Email: **enquiries@rothesgolfclub.co.uk**
Website: **www.rothesgolfclub.co.uk**
Terrain: **Parkland**

Length m **4,972**	Length l **4,874**
Par/SSS m **68/64**	Par/SSS l **68/69**
Rec m **62**	Rec l **64**
Par 3 m **2**	Par 3 l **2**
Par 5 m **0**	Par 5 l **1**

Signature Hole: Sixth, PAR 3 over a gulley onto a long narrow green.

Captain's Hole: Fourth, PAR 3.

Times to Avoid: Saturday and Sunday mornings.

Clubhouse: Opened 2000, Catering and Bar also changing rooms with showers.

Condition: Tidy course with small greens and light rough.

Memorabilia: Ball markers, hats and pitch forks. Clothing to order.

Wildlife: Birds of Prey, deer and squirrels.

Location: Centre of village, on the road past 13th century castle wall.

Accommodation: Seafield, Ben Aigen, and Eastbank Hotels.

Lost ball: 3

Comments: A very friendly club with spectacular views over the Spey Valley, a testing short course. Good catering facilities.

Fame: Terry Wogan

Discount: Moray for Golf

Clubs visiting: Contact club in writing, telephone or e-mail.

Caps visiting: Advance notice

C B T CHR SHW CTR D

127
Covesea Links

Est: 1902

Duffus, Lossiemouth, Moray, IV30 5QS
Contact: **The Secretary**
Email: **info@covesealinks.com**
Website: **www.covesealinks.com**
Terrain: **Parkland**
Length m **3,066** (12 holes)
Par/SSS m **36/36**
Par 3 m **9**
Par 5 m **0**

Location: Two miles west of Lossiemouth on B9040

CH T

challenge for any golfer. The seventh in particular is a lovely hole with gorgeous views across the course and the Moray Firth, while visitors are invited to take advantage of the seat at the tenth to rest their feet and consider the challenges to come.

A few hundred yards along the road is the Golf Dedication Centre with a driving range and the Wee Links Golf Course, a nine-hole PAR 3 course.

Close by the famous whisky distilleries of Glenfiddich, Glenfarclas and Glenlivet and surrounded by majestic hills is **128 Ballindalloch Castle** Golf Course which is a relatively new course, first played in 2002. Designed by Donald Steel and Tom Mackenzie this is another of those special courses with 18 tees serving nine holes, making a second round a very different experience. The first nine is 3,229 yards from the yellow tees and has two PAR 5's, two PAR 3's, and a PAR of 36. Set on the banks of the river Avon and close by the Spey, this is an interesting layout in beautiful surroundings. The signature hole, seventh, is a PAR 3 with its green situated on the banks of the Avon and offers a challenging test of iron play.

Finally in this tour we come to Kinloss which has its own claim to fame. Many of the courses reviewed here boast an 18 hole course with the nine-holer as an additional feature. Kinloss is unique in that it has two nine-hole courses. **129 Course 1** is a gently undulating layout offering enjoyable but challenging play together with magnificent panoramic views across the Moray Firth to the distant Caithness mountains. **130 Course 2** is longer and more challenging, demanding the concentration of the more experienced golfer.

128
Ballindalloch Castle

Est: 2002

Tel: **01807 500305**

Lagmore, Ballindalloch, Banffshire, AB37 9AA
Contact: **The Secretary**
Email: **golf@ballindallochcastle.co.uk**
Website: **www.ballindallochcastle.co.uk**
Terrain: **Parkland**

Length m **6,495**	Length l **5,593**
Par/SSS m **71/70**	
Par 3 m **2**	Par 3 l **2**
Par 5 m **2**	Par 5 l **2**

Signature Hole: Seventh, 188 yard PAR 3 'Tall Pines', green position on the bank of the River Avon provides for a challenging test of short iron play.

129
Kinloss Course 1

Est: Unknown

Tel: **01343 850585**

Kinloss, Forres, Morayshire, IV36 2UB
Contact: **The Secretary**
Email: **info@kinlossgolf.co.uk**
Website: **www.kinlossgolf.co.uk**
Terrain: **Parkland**
Length m **4,822**
Par/SSS m **68/68**
Par 3 m **4**
Par 5 m **1**

Location: Five miles east of Forres on the B9089

C B BG CH T CHR CTR PG
D P S

130
Kinloss Course 2

Est: Unknown

Tel: **01343 850585**

Kinloss, Forres, Morayshire, IV36 2UB
Contact: **The Secretary**
Email: **info@kinlossgolf.co.uk**
Website: **www.kinlossgolf.co.uk**
Terrain: **Parkland**
Length m **5,528**
Par/SSS m **70/70**
Par 3 m **2**
Par 5 m **1**

CH CTR

Tobermory Golf Club third green

SOUTH EAST
Edinburgh, Lothians and the Borders

Embracing Edinburgh, the Lothians and the Borders, the South East of Scotland is not only the cultural and administrative centre of the country but is also the cradle of golf. Of the 23 courses in the area featured in this guide 15 have an Edinburgh post code, emphasising the important role the game plays in the life of the Capital. Golf, or Gowf as it once was known, has been played in the area since the 14th century and the sport was first recognised in 1502. James IV tried to ban the game before becoming a convert and another royal to become a keen player was Mary Queen of Scots who is believed to have played at Musselburgh Links, the world's oldest playing course, in 1567.

The Pentland, Moorfoot and Lammermuir Hills are important geographical features of the South East of Scotland and their influence is recognisable in the terrain of many of the courses, while others have the town and coastal features of parkland and links layouts. So there is something for everyone in our nine-hole golf courses of the South East.

131 Ravelston, the course closest to the centre of Edinburgh, was established in 1912, stretches over 5,218 yards and has a PAR/SSS of 66. It is a parkland course to the NW of Corstorphine Hill, where, despite its city environment, foxes, badgers and birds of prey can often be seen. Amongst the more difficult holes is the signature second, a 236 yard PAR 3 played to a raised green guarded by bunkers. The Captain points to the enjoyable seventh where a tight drive is needed to reach the prime position on the fairway for the second to a narrow green. At weekends Ravelston is open only to members and their guests.

Also close to the City centre is **132 The Prince's Course** a municipal course set in heathland amidst the scenic Braid Hills and with panoramic views of Edinburgh. Facilities include a driving range and pro

---

131 Ravelston

Est: 1912

Tel: **0131 3152486**

24 Ravelston Dykes Road, Edinburgh, EH4 3NZ
Contact: **Jim Lowrie**
Email: **ravelstongc@hotmail.com**
Website: **www.ravelstongolfclub.com**
Terrain: **Hilly parkland course on NW side of Corstorphine Hill**

Length m **5,170**	Length l **5,020**
Par/SSS m **66/66**	Par/SSS l **70/69**
Rec m **64**	
Par 3 m **3**	Par 3 l **2**
Par 5 m **0**	Par 5 l **1**

Signature Hole: Second, 236 yard PAR 3 raised green guarded by bunkers

Captain's Hole: Seventh, tight drive to prime fairways position then to a narrow green. Overshoot at your peril.

Times to Avoid: Weekends, members guests only

Clubhouse: Small dining room with intimate atmosphere.

Condition: Prime playing condition

Wildlife: Foxes, badgers and birds of prey

Location: On the A90 to the north west of Edinburgh

Accommodation: Several B & B's nearby

Lost ball: 2

Comments: A challenging course, always in excellent condition. Will test a players short game.

Fame: Sir Sean Connery

Caps visiting: Contact Secretary

C CHR CTR PG

132
Braid Hills – The Prince's Course

Est: Unknown

Tel: **0131 4473568**

22, Braid Hills Approach, Edinburgh, EH10 6JY
Contact: **The Secretary**
Email:
 info.braidhills@edinburghleisure.co.uk
Website: **www.edinburghleisuregolf.co.uk**
Terrain: **Heathland**
Length m **4,012**
Par/SSS m **62/62**
Par 3 m **5**
Par 5 m **0**
Location: On A702 south of Edinburgh city
 centre

C CH T CTR P S

Portobello Clubhouse and Golf Course

shop. The course measures 4,012 yards and has a PAR of 62. Find it on the A702 south of the city centre.

Another course under development in the Braids Hill area is the unique 12 hole **133 Hermitage Family** course, specially designed to cater for children and disabled people. This project commenced in 2000 and, under the patronage of Ryder Cup player Andrew Coltart, will provide a suitable and safe environment for 5 to 12 year old children and the disabled to participate in golf. It is a 'not for profit' enterprise and is supported by Sport Scotland, Edinburgh Council, the Royal and Ancient Golf Club of St Andrews and the Scottish Golf Union.

As part of the major **134 Swanston** New Golf Course centre the PAR 3 nine-hole Templar Course benefits from a full range of outstanding golf facilities. On the outskirts of Edinburgh overlooked by the Pentland Hills it was originally laid out in 1928 as a nine-hole ladies course, although this later became an 18 hole course and the new nine-holer was built in 2005. It has been designed as a course where youngsters and beginners can improve without pressure from impatient seniors. There is a driving range, three practice greens and no less than four PGA professionals.

At **135 Portobello** is a parkland pay-and-play course enjoying lovely views of Arthur's Seat. This is an open, well-presented and maintained course with forgiving fairways while the small, tight greens

Hermitage Family

133
Hermitage Family

Est: 2008

Tel: **0131 4475700**

11 Braid Hills Drive, Edinburgh, EH10 6GZ
Contact: **The Secretary**
Email: **hermitage@aiscotland.org.uk**
Website: **www.hermitagescotland.co.uk**
Terrain: **Inland**
Length m **3,702**
Par/SSS m **47** 12 holes
Par 3 m **3** (12 holes)
Par 5 m **2** (12 holes)

134
Swanston

Est: 2005

Tel: **0131 445 2239**

Swanston Templar Short Course
111 Swanston Road, Edinburgh, EH10 7DS
Contact: **Owen Leslie**
Email: **golf@swanston.co.uk**
Website: **www.swanstongolf.co.uk**
Terrain: **Parkland**
Length: circa **2,800 yards**
Par/SSS **54/54**
Par 3s **9**
Par 5 **0**

Clubhouse: Very modern clubhouse with full facilities including pro-shop, brasserie and a lovely terrace.

Condition: Full time green keepers mean the course is in excellent condition

Location: South side of Edinburgh, close to the Pentland Hills. Leave the Edinburgh bypass, A720 at the Fairmilehead Junction.

Lost ball rating: 1 or 2

Secretary's Comments: The Templar Course was created in 2005 as a childrens and beginners course.

**C B CH T CHR SWH CTR
PG D P S**

135
Portobello

Est: Unknown

Tel: **0131 6694361**

Stanley Street, Portobello, Edinburgh, EH15 1JJ
Contact: **The Secretary**
Email:
   info.portobello@edinburghleisure.co.uk
Website: **www.edinburghleisuregolf.co.uk**
Terrain: **Parkland**
Length m **4,504**
Par/SSS m **64/64**
Par 3 m **4**
Par 5 m **0**
Location: Four miles east of Edinburgh

B CH T CTR D

Whitehill House Golf Course

demand accurate approach shots. The course plays over 4,504 yards to a PAR of 64. Most players enjoy the signature ninth, a 177 yards PAR 3 requiring a long straight drive avoiding bunkers at 150 yards and then to a sloping green.

At Dundas Estate a mile south of South Queensferry is the **136 Dundas Park** course established in 1957 and measuring 6,104 yards. The PAR/SSS is 70/69. This is a quiet parkland course with a small clubhouse and some commanding views. This is particularly true at the sixth where the elevated tee looks out over the whole course and the surrounding countryside.

Another quiet course in the vicinity of Edinburgh is **137 Gogarburn** a 12 hole Parkland layout situated just off the Edinburgh–Glasgow A8 road and close to the City airport. This is a parkland course with beautiful views of the Midlothian scenery.

From Gogarburn the route to **138 Kingsfield** heads south on the A8 and links to the M9. Situated close to Linlithgow, just off the motorway, Kingsfield is a new nine-holer with unusually good facilities. These include a driving range, golf tuition studios, access to seven PGA professionals, a clubhouse and coffee shop and links with the famous nearby Champneys Inn which offer a Golfer's Steak Experience! This is a USGA standard course extending to nearly 3,000 yards.

The **139 Bridgend and District** golf course, formerly known as Haughburn, is situated in the heart of West Lothian with commanding views north to the Firth of Forth and the Kingdom of Fife. The course was opened for play in 1998 although it was founded

136
Dundas Park

Est: 1957

Tel: **0131 3191347**

Dundas Estate, South Queensferry, West Lothian, EH30 9SS
Contact: **Jimmy Wood**
Email: **cmkwood@btinternet.com**
Website: **www.dundasparkgolf.co.uk**
Terrain: **Parkland**

Length m **6,104**	Length l **5,498**
Par/SSS m **70/69**	Par/SSS l 72/71
Rec m **62**	
Par 3 m 2	Par 3 l 2
Par 5 m 1	Par 5 l 2

Captain's Hole: Sixth, tee gives excellent views over course and surrounding countryside. A 420 yard dog-leg, it requires an accurate tee shot and precise second to reach the green.

Times to Avoid: Weekends

Clubhouse: Small clubhouse. No bar or catering without prior notice

Condition: Parkland turf.

Wildlife: Pheasants, deer and hares.

Location: Approach from A8000. Dundas Estate one mile south of South Queensferry.

Accommodation: Hawes Inn, South Queensferry

Lost ball: 2

Comments: Very quiet with good views

Clubs visiting: Contact Secretary

Caps visiting: Contact Secretary for free round

C CHR

The Prince's Course putting out

137
Gogarburn

Est: 1975

Tel: **0131 3334718**

Hanley Lodge, Rodinlaw Road, Newbridge, Gogarburn, EH28 8NN
Contact: **The Secretary**
Email: **enquiries@gogarburngc.co.uk**
Website: **www.gogarburngc.com**
Terrain: **Parkland**
Length m **3,030** (12 holes)
Par/SSS m **43/64**
Par 3 m **3**
Par 5 m **0**
Location: Adjacent to Edinburgh Airport slip road off A8

C B T CHR SHW CTR PG P

138
Kingsfield

Est. 2009

Tel: **01506 671 607**

Kingsfield Golf Centre, Linlithgow, EH49 7LS
Email: **info@kingsfieldgolf.com**
Website: **www.kingsfieldgolf.com**
Terrain: **Inland Links**
Length: **2,857 yards**
Par/SSS: **68/67**
Clubhouse: Good facilities including the Tee Caddy coffee shop.
Condition: USGA spec greens provide perfect putting surfaces all year.
Location: Close to the M8 at Linlithgow
Lost ball rating: 1 or 2

C CH T CHR SHW CTR PG D P S

139
Bridgend and District

Est: 1998

Tel: **01506 834140**

Willowdean, Bridgend, Linlithgow, EH49 6NW
Contact: **The Secretary**
Email: **bridgendgolfclub@virgin.net**
Website: **www.bridgendgolfclub.com**
Terrain: **Parkland**
Length m **5,451**
Par/SSS m **67/66**
Par 3 m **2**
Par 5 m **0**
Location: Two and a half miles east of Linlithgow

C B BG T SHW CTR P

Gifford Clubhouse

several years before by a group of determined villagers who recognised a need for a course in the area. It is built on the abandoned shale oil mine and now offers an enjoyable test of golf. With a parkland nature the course is 5,451 yards long and has a PAR/SSS of 67/66.

Ask the secretary of **140 Oatridge** Golf Course why his course is worth a visit and his prompt response is; 'A friendly welcome, lovely scenery and the course is in excellent condition'. This is clearly a message heeded by Bernard Gallacher, one of the more famous players to enjoy a round. Established in 2000 this is a parkland course with streams and mature trees at Ecclesmachan, three miles from Broxburn, West Lothian on the B8046. The signature third is a special treat. It is a driveable PAR 4 with pond, stream and a large oak tree guarding the green, while the Captain invites you to play his favourite, the final hole, a gentle PAR 4 to an inviting green with 'Binny Craig' as a backdrop.

141 Polkemmet is unusually long for a nine-hole course at 6,442 yards and a PAR/SSS of 74. Now a Council Park centre, the course was created in 1981 and is based within the grounds of an old private estate. There is a 15 bay driving range and a number of facilities apart from golf. Mature woodland and well established rhododendrons add to the attractions and the River Almond features on a number of holes. A wide range of birds can be seen here including buzzards. The signature hole is the ninth with a tee shot across the river to a tree ringed green.

The **142 Old Links** at Musselburgh was originally a seven hole course with another hole added in 1835 and the full nine-holes coming into play in 1870. Possibly the most famous nine-hole course in the world, with a wonderful history, this should be a place of pilgrimage for every lover of nine-hole golf courses. As would be expected the course is in first class condition and every hole has its own history and challenge. The names of the second and third holes, 'The Graves' and 'Barracks Entry' tell a story

140 Oatridge

Est: 2000

Tel: **01506 859636**

West Binny Road, Ecclesmachan, West Lothian, EH52 6NR

Contact: **Brian Inglis**

Email: **jthomson@oatridge.ac.uk**

Website: **www.oatridge.ac.uk**

Terrain: **Parkland with streams and mature trees**

Length m **5,540**	Length l **5,120**
Par/SSS m **69/67**	Par/SSS l **72/73**
Rec m **67**	Rec l **74**
Par 3 m **2**	Par 3 l **1**
Par 5 m **1**	Par 5 l **1**

Signature Hole: Third, driveable PAR 4 with pond, stream and large oak tree guarding the green.

Captain's Hole: Ninth, gentle PAR 4 to an inviting green with 'Binny Craig' as a backdrop.

Clubhouse: Changing rooms and some catering.

Condition: First Class

Memorabilia: Yes

Wildlife: Buzzards, hawks, etc.

Location: In village of Ecclesmachan

Accommodation: Houston House Hotel, Uphall.

Lost ball: 2

Comments: Friendly welcome, lovely scenery and course in excellent condition.

Fame: Bernard Gallacher

Caps visiting: Contact Secretary

C BG T CHR CTR PG P

C Clubhouse **B** Bar **BG** Buggy **CH** Club Hire **T** Trolley **CHR** Changing Rooms **SHW** Showers

141 Polkemmet

Est: 1981

Tel: **01501 743 905**

Council Park Centre, Whitburn, Polkemmet, EH47 0AD
Contact: **J.B. Fleming**
Email: **polkemmet@westlothian.gov.uk**
Website: **www.beecraigs.com**
Terrain: **Wooded parkland**
Length m **6,442**   Length l **6,442**
Par/SSS m **74/74**
Par 3 m **1**
Par 5 m **2**

Signature Hole: Ninth, tee shot across the river to a tree ringed green.

Clubhouse: Café and bar facilities and toilets

Condition: Very good

Wildlife: Wide range of birds including buzzards

Location: Just off M8 mid way between Whitburn and Harthill on B7066

Accommodation: Hillcroft Hotel Whitburn

Lost ball: 7

Comments: Inexpensive, long and interesting course

C B T

142 Musselburgh – Old Links

Est: 1870 (Nine hole course)

Tel: **0131 6655438**

The Old Course, Balcarres Road, Musselburgh, Nr Edinburgh, EH21 7SD
Contact: **The Secretary**
Email: **oldlinks@enjoyleisure.com**
Website: **www.musselburgholdlinks.co.uk**
Terrain: **Links**
Length m **5,774**   Length l **5,330**
Par/SSS m **68/68**   Par/SSS l **71/71**
Par 3 m **3**   Par 3 l **2**
Par 5 m **1**   Par 5 l **1**

Signature Hole: Fifth, 'The Sea Hole' PAR 3

Location: Signposted from the A1 and the A720 Edinburgh by-pass

C B CH T CHR SHW CTR D P S

of the military history of the area while 'Mrs Forman's Hole' is named after an old inn where early golfers were passed refreshments as they played. The fifth is possibly the most famous hole, and has been copied and incorporated into many other courses.

We would probably not go as far as 'Golf World' who described **143 Gifford** golf course as 'the best nine-holes in Scotland' but it is a beautiful, superbly maintained course situated on the edge of the East Lothian village some 30 minutes from Edinburgh on the B6355. Nestling in its tranquil setting at the foot of the Lammermuir Hills the course is set in parkland bounded by mature woods and farmland. The Speedy Burn flows through the course and comes into play on several of the holes. This is quite a long course at 6,050 yards and the greens are renowned for their quality and difficulty. We recommend the signature ninth, a 473 yard PAR 5 which with a following wind can be reached in two shots. That is if you can carry a burn, avoid the trees and keep out of the rough! Perhaps the PAR 4 396 yard sixth, the Captain's favourite, will be more to your liking, even though there are still problems with three bunkers protecting the green with gorse behind.

Situated in the Esk Valley and enjoying panoramic views, the **144 Melville** golf course at Lasswade, just three miles from the Edinburgh bypass, is a short and challenging parkland course. Laid out over 4,604 yards the course has twisting fairways and cunningly placed bunkers with excellent greens. An additional attraction is the floodlit driving range.

Just off the Edinburgh by-pass through Lasswade is the historic **145 Whitehill House** with its glorious and testing PAR 70 nine-hole layout. In a mature woodland setting there is a good combination of long and short PAR 4 and PAR 5 holes with tricky dog-legs to negotiate and with three challenging PAR 3 holes. The signature hole is the PAR 3 eighth, 'Ramsey's Revenge' where a tee shot from an elevated tee plays across a wooded gorge to an undulating green surrounded by bunkers.

143
Gifford

Est: 1904

Tel: **01620 810591**

Edinburgh Road, Gifford, Nr. Haddington, EH41 4JE
Contact: **Robert Stewart**
Email: **secretary@giffordgolfclub.com**
Website: **www.giffordgolfclub.com**
Terrain: **Rolling parkland**

Length m **6,050**	Length l **5,694**
Par/SSS m **71/69**	Par/SSS l **73/73**
Rec m **63**	Rec l **67**
Par 3 m **2**	Par 3 l **2**
Par 5 m **1**	Par 5 l **2**

Signature Hole: Ninth, PAR 5

Captain's Hole: Sixth, PAR 4

Location: South-west of Gifford, five miles from Haddington.

C BG T CHR SHW CTR PG

144
Melville

Est: 1995

Tel: **0131 6638038**

Melville Golf Centre, Lasswade, Midlothian, EH18 1AN
Contact: **Colin MacFarlane**
Email: **golf@melvillegolf.co.uk**
Website: **www.melvillegolf.co.uk**
Terrain: **Parkland**

Length m **4,604**	Length l **3,834**
Par/SSS m **66/66**	Par/SSS l **66/66**
Par 3 m **4**	Par 3 l **4**
Par 5 m **1**	Par 5 l **1**

Times to Avoid: Saturday mornings and summer evenings

Clubhouse: Vended drinks and snacks

Condition: Well maintained with excellent greens

Memorabilia: Yes

Wildlife: Deer, foxes and variety of birds

Location: On the A7 Galashiels Road sign-posted from Edinburgh City bypass

Accommodation: Laird and Dog, Lasswade, Dalhousie Castle Hotel, Bonnyrigg, Melville Castle Hotel, Lasswade.

Lost ball: 1

Comments: Short but challenging parkland course with excellent greens. Lies in the Esk Valley with panoramic views.

Clubs visiting: Discounts for groups

C CH T CHR SHW CTR PG D P S

145
Whitehill House

Est: Unknown

Tel: **0131 2202440**

Whitehill House, Rosewell, Midlothian, EH24 9EG
Contact: **The Secretary**
Email: **mail@businessparcs.com**
Website: **www.whitehillhousegolf.com**
Terrain: **Woodland**

Length m **6,324**
Par/SSS m **70**
Par 3 m **3**
Par 5 m **1**

Signature Hole: Eighth, 187 yard PAR 3 'Ramsey's Revenge' played over a wooded gorge to an undulating green surrounded by bunkers.

C

Whitehill House ninth Green

146 Vogrie golf course is a municipal course set in a country park at Gorebridge south-east of Edinburgh on the B6372 just off the A68. Other facilities here include an adventure play area, garden centre, barbecue sites and woodland paths. This parkland course measures 5,060 yards and the PAR/SSS is 66.

Our search for nine-hole courses now takes us further from Edinburgh and into the Borders where our first course, **147 Innerleithen**, is situated at Leithen Water on the B709 Heriot road. Enjoying lovely views of the surrounding hills there is a stream meandering through six holes of this flat, parkland style course. The signature hole here is the first, a PAR 3, 177 yard challenge, with a narrow entry to the green, a roadway on the right, a burn to the front left, and the Leithen Water at the back.

On the A68 some half a mile from Lauder and around 26 miles south of Edinburgh is the Royal Burgh of **148 Lauder** Golf Club and one of the finest nine-hole courses in the Borders. The course was opened in 1896 to a design by Willie Park Jnr., British Champion 1887/1889 who holds the pro record of 70, which has stood since 1905. It is a moorland, undulating course of 6,050 yards and PAR/SSS 72/69. Noted for its excellent greens and generously wide fairways the signature hole is the PAR 3 sixth 'Quarry Hole' with a blind tee shot, and the Captain's choice is the PAR 4 fourth with a dog-leg to the left. Non-golfing members of your party might want to keep an eye open for tawny owls, cuckoos, sparrowhawks and roe deer.

Elsewhere in this guide I have had a bit of a moan about the moves at some fine nine-holers to 'upgrade' to an 18 hole course. Well at last I have something to crow about on this front; a course which has gone in the opposite direction. **149 Galashiels** Golf Club downsized to a 9 hole course with a new layout in April 2009. Interestingly, when the course was established in 1885 to a James Braid design it was

146
Vogrie

Est: Unknown
Tel: **01875 821716**
Vogrie Estate Country Park, Gorebridge, Edinburgh, EH23 4NU
Contact: **The Secretary**
Email: **ian.welsh@midlothian.gov.uk**
Website: **www.midlothian.gov.uk**
Terrain: **Parkland**
Length m **5,060**
Par/SSS m **66/66**
Par 3 m **3**
Par 5 m **0**
Location: On B6372 off A68, south-east of Edinburgh

T CHR CTR

147
Innerleithen

Est: Unknown

Tel: 01896 830951

Leithen Water, Leithen Road, Innerleithen,
EH44 6NL
Contact: **The Secretary**
Email: **contact@innerleithengolf.co.uk**
Website: **www.innerleithengolf.co.uk**
Terrain: **Parkland**
Length m **6,066**
Par/SSS m **70/69**
Par 3 m **3**
Par 5 m **2**
Location: In the Leithen Valley, six miles from
Peebles on the B709 Heriot Road

**C B CH T CHR SHW CTR
PG P**

148
Lauder

Est: 1896

Tel: 01578 722240

Galashiels Road, Lauder, Berwickshire, TD2 6RS
Contact: **Mr R. Towers.**
Email: **secretary@laudergolfclub.co.uk**
Website: **www.laudergolfclub.co.uk**
Terrain: **Moorland, undulating, wonderful
views of the Lauderdale District**

Length m **6,050**	Length l **5,193**
Par/SSS m **72/69**	Par/SSS l **73/71**
Rec m **66**	
Par 3 m **3**	Par 3 l **3**
Par 5 m **3**	Par 5 l **4**

Signature Hole: Sixth, PAR 3 quarry hole, blind
tee shot.

Captain's Hole: Fourth, PAR 4, dog-leg left.

Times to Avoid: Monday and Wednesday from
5.30–6.30pm, Sunday before noon.

Clubhouse: Basic changing facilities.

Condition: Excellent fairways/greens. Well
drained.

Wildlife: Tawny owls, cuckoos, sparrowhawks
and roe deer.

Location: A68 south of Edinburgh signposted
to Galasheils at Town Hall; past the Cemetery
on rhs about a quarter mile from Lauder.

Accommodation: The Black Bull Hotel, The
Carfraemill Hotel, The Eagle Inn and The
Lauderdale Hotel.

Lost ball: 2

Comments: Considered by visitors to be one
of the best nine-holes in the area. Stunning
views, excellent greens and generous width
of fairways.

Fame: Designed by W. Park (Jnr) British
Champion 1887/1889; holds the Pro record
of 70.

Clubs visiting: For groups of six. By prior
arrangement discounts for more than 15.

C CHR PG P

149
Galashiels

Est: 1884

Tel: 01896 753 724

Ladhope Recreation Ground, Galashiels,
TD1 2NJ
Contact: **The Secretary**
Email: **secretary@galashiels-golfclub.co.uk**
Website: **www.galashiels-golfclub.co.uk**

Winter Rules

Please note the following rules to
be observed over the winter
period and until further notice.

Since the grass does not grow in
winter on the fairways, players
should move their ball each time
from where they land on the
fairway to the nearest point of
semi-rough at edge of fairway on
the closest side and no nearer
the hole at no cost penalty.

The ball may then be played
from that spot.

a nine holer, then increased to 18 holes in 1912. For some time the members have felt that the notorious 10th hole was deterring players so now it has been dumped in the dustbin of history in favour of a more user-friendly layout.

The course still enjoys fabulous views over the town and the Border hills and there are demanding holes to tempt the most avid golfer. Congratulations to Galashiels for this courageous move which should increase the numbers playing and control the ever rising cost of maintenance.

Moving further south down the A68 and into country known for rugby as much as golf, the next course is **150 Melrose** a parkland course set in beautiful scenery at the foot of the Eildon Hills, whose triple peaks are the most distinctive landmark in the Borders. This is an attractive course with well tended greens and tree-lined fairways. The feature hole is the PAR 4 eighth played over 414 yards with a second shot to a green guarded by four bunkers. A clubhouse offers changing rooms, showers and a licensed bar.

A few miles south and just a quarter of a mile off the A68 on the B6404 is the **151 St Boswells** course, which plays down to the River Tweed. This is described as an 'easy amble' but is not without its difficulties as there are plenty of trees and the river to negotiate, all in a lovely setting. The signature hole is the second played from a plateau tee to a large green surrounded by bunkers and a drop to the third fairway. The sixth, which is the Captain's choice, is a PAR 4 where an accurate second shot is needed to a green surrounded on three sides by water. All facilities are available in the newly refurbished clubhouse which has great views of the River Tweed and where water fowl, deer and salmon can be spotted.

Also close to the A68 and a little further south is the **152 Lilliardsedge** course between Ancrum and St Boswells. This is a peacefully situated course in outstanding condition set in 75 acres of gently rolling

C Clubhouse B Bar BG Buggy CH Club Hire T Trolley CHR Changing Rooms SHW Showers

150
Melrose

Est: 1880

Tel: **01896 822855**

Dingleton Road, Melrose, TD6 9HS
Contact: **Les. Wallace**
Email: **melrosegolfclub@tiscali.co.uk**
Website: **www.melrosegolfclub.co.uk**
Terrain: **Tree-lined Parkland**

Length m **5,562**	Length l **4,996**
Par/SSS m **70/68**	Par/SSS l **72/70**
Rec m 62	Rec l 71
Par 3 m 2	Par 3 l 2
Par 5 m 0	Par 5 l 0

Signature Hole: Fourth, dog-leg tee shot laying up to a water hazard. Second shot requires accurate approach to an elevated tee.

Captain's Hole: Ninth, lay up from tee short of stream and ponds guarding greens

Times to Avoid: Saturdays and Tuesdays

Clubhouse: Changing rooms with showers, bar

Condition: Usually good. Best between May to September

Memorabilia: Yes

Wildlife: Course attracts much wildlife.

Location: At foot of Eildon Hills on A68 south from Edinburgh

Accommodation: Melrose Burts Hotel and Townhouse Hotel

Lost ball: 1/2

Comments: Beautiful scenery

151
St Boswells

Est: 1899

Tel: **01835 823527**

Braeheads, St. Boswells, Melrose, TD6 0DE
Contact: **Graham Philips**
Email: **secretary@stboswellsgolfclub.co.uk**
Website: **www.stboswellsgolfclub.co.uk**
Terrain: **Parkland**

Length m **5,274**	Length l **4,910**
Par/SSS m **68/66**	Par/SSS l **70/68**
Rec m 61	Rec l 70
Par 3 m 3	Par 3 l 3
Par 5 m 1	Par 5 l 2

Signature Hole: Second, plateau tee to a large green surrounded by bunkers and drop to third fairway. Great views.

Captain's Hole: Sixth, PAR 4 accurate second shot necessary to a green surrounded on three sides by water.

Times to Avoid: Evenings and some weekends

Clubhouse: Newly refurbished with all facilities and great views to river Tweed.

Condition: Good

Memorabilia: Ball markers

Wildlife: Water fowl, deer, salmon

Location: Off A68 into St Boswells village at the Buccleuch Arms Hotel, carry on to end of village then a left into a narrow entrance signposted before right hand bend.

Accommodation: Buccleuch Arms Hotel, and wide choice in Melrose.

Lost ball: 3

Comments: The course plays down to the River Tweed and is a pleasant amble but not altogether easy. Plenty of trees and a river to negotiate in a very special setting.

Discount: Scottish Borders Freedom of Fairways, two for one

Clubs visiting: Contact Secretary

Caps visiting: Contact Secretary

152
Lilliardsedge

Est: 1999

Tel: **01835 830271**

Lilliardsedge, Jedburgh, TD8 6TZ
Contact: **Brian Wetherley**
Email: **info@bordercaravans.co.uk**
Website: **www.lilliardsedgepark.co.uk**
Terrain: **Parkland**

Length m **5,386**	Length l **4,976**
Par/SSS m **70/68**	Par/SSS l **72/72**
Rec m 66	
Par 3 m 2	Par 3 l 2
Par 5 m 1	Par 5 l 2

Signature Hole: Fourth, 253 yards PAR 4 'Hill Top'. Extensive views and gentle slope to local hills and mausoleum

Captain's Hole: Ninth, water hole dog-leg right, beware the rough

Times to Avoid: Saturday and Sunday mornings

Clubhouse: Yes, small friendly bar and food available at weekends and special golf outings

Condition: Possibly the best greens in the borders

Memorabilia: Ball markers, pitch repairers and polo shirts

Wildlife: Red squirrels

Location: On A68 six miles north of Jedburgh

Accommodation: Caravan hire at Lilliardsedge and Riverside, Hawick. Tourers welcome

Lost ball: 3

Comments: Outstanding condition of course

Fame: Many

Discount: two for one

Clubs visiting: By arrangement

C B T CHR SHW CTR

C B T CHR SHW CTR

C B BG CH T CHR SHW CTR PG P

---

landscaped grounds which makes full use of the natural features. Every hole has its own difficulties with bunkers, trees, water hazards and out-of-bounds all waiting for the wayward shot. The clubhouse doubles as a bar and entertainment centre for the holiday park.

A few miles to the west and a mile south of the town on the A7 is the moorland **153 Selkirk** golf course, set on the side of Selkirk Hill. This is yet another exceptionally scenic facility with undulating heather, gorse-lined fairways and well maintained greens. The 518 yard PAR 5 eighth is the signature hole demanding a drive into a narrow fairway flanked by heather slopes. The second shot sets up the approach to the green which is hidden behind grassy mounds.

A refreshingly frank official website describes the **154 Lilliesleaf** golf course as a 'fun course for the less discerning golfer where dogs and children are all welcome.' In fact this is quite a long course at 5,072 yards with a PAR of 68, where there are plenty of hazards awaiting the unwary golfer including trees, water and bunkers. This course is a little south of Selkirk and two miles east of the A7 on B6400 signposted to Synton, but is tucked away deep in the countryside and is not easy to find.

The next course on our tour used to be Jedburgh, sitting above the town in a truly lovely situation. Sadly it has been 'improved' to 18 holes and no longer features on our agenda. All too often these 'improvements' mean a mediocre 18 holer instead of a truly beautiful nine-hole course. Maintenance becomes more difficult and expensive, resources become stretched, membership and green fees rise and many older members become disaffected. Hopefully this will not happen at Jedburgh.

Our final point of call in the south east is **155 Newcastleton** in Liddesdale. This historic town, on the B6357, was founded in 1793 by the Duke of Buccleuch as a handloom weaving centre and a visit

153 Selkirk

Est: 1883

Tel: **01750 720261**

Selkirk Hill, Selkirk, Scottish Borders, TD7 4NW

Contact: **Jim Hay**

Email: **secretary@selkirkgolfclub.co.uk**

Website: **www.selkirkgolfclub.co.uk**

Terrain: **Heathland**

Length m **5,575**	Length l **4,870**
Par/SSS m **68/68**	Par/SSS l **69/69**
Rec m **60**	Rec l **66**
Par 3 m **3**	Par 3 l **3**
Par 5 m **1**	Par 5 l **1**

Signature Hole: Eighth, 518 yards popular with low handicappers tough test for others. Narrow landing area

Captain's Hole: Fourth, easy tee shot with a good chance of making the green in two shots.

Times to Avoid: Weekends

Clubhouse: Friendly with bar, changing rooms and showers

Condition: Greens especially good

Wildlife: Wide range of bird-life, kites, stoats, rabbits

Location: Leaving Selkirk Market Place on the A7 towards Hawick, 100 metres from 30 mile stone

Accommodation: Plenty good hotels, restaurants and self catering

Lost ball: 3

Comments: Warm welcome for visitors

Discount: Freedom of Scotland (Visit Scotland)

Clubs visiting: Contact Secretary

Caps visiting: Free if notified

C B CHR SHW PG P

154
Lilliesleaf

Est: 2000

Tel: **01835 870333**

Dimpleknowe, Lilliesleaf, Melrose, TD6 9JU
Contact: **Norman Cameron**
Email: **norman@dimpleknow.com**
Website: **www.dimpleknowe.co.uk/golf**
Terrain: **Farm and woodland with water
    feature**

Length m **5,180**	Length l **4,360**
Par/SSS m **68/68**	
Rec m **37** (9 holes)	
Par 3 m **3**	Par 3 l **3**
Par 5 m **1**	Par 5 l **1**

Signature Hole: Third, PAR 3 high tee over burn,
    green in old quarry

Captain's Hole: Eighth, PAR 4 from elevated tee
    through narrow wood. Green with pond
    behind – drop zone on island in pond.

Clubhouse: Basic

Condition: No frills

Wildlife: Buzzards, linnets, deer, hares

Location: On B road between Synton and
    Lillisleaf north of Hawick. Two miles east
    of the A7

Accommodation: Two en-suite self catering
    cottages on site. Three pubs within two miles.

Lost ball: 5

Comments: Very relaxed, children welcome

Clubs visiting: £100 per day up to 20 players

C BG CH T CHR PG P

155
Newcastleton

Est: 1894

Tel: **013873 75608**

Holm Hill, Newcastleton, Borders, TD9 0QD
Contact: **George A. Wilson**
Website: **www.visitscottishborders.com**
Terrain: **Parkland, partly hilly**

Length m **5,491**	Length l **5,491**
Par/SSS m **69/70**	
Rec m **67**	Rec l **74**
Par 3 m **2**	Par 3 l **2**
Par 5 m **1**	Par 5 l **1**

Clubhouse: Changing rooms open on
    competition days.

Condition: Good

Wildlife: Deer and buzzards

Location: North from Carlisle on A7 to
    Canonbie. Twenty miles south of Hawick.

Accommodation: Grapes Hotel

Comments: A challenging course

Clubs visiting: Contact Secretary

C CHR PG

Guthrie Castle Golf Course

Starter's Hut, Musselburgh Old Course

to the nearby Hermitage Castle should not be missed. The course is set on the side of Holm Hill with lovely views over the Liddesdale hills and the small greens offer a good test for players of all abilities. There are 12 tees serving the nine holes which means that several holes play differently the second time round. This is true of the ninth which becomes a PAR 5 on the second round and is known as the signature hole for the course. It is a 521 yards downhill tee shot with a dog-leg approach to a small green hidden below a bank.

Putting out at Newcastleton Golf Course

ISLANDS
From the Clyde to the Shetlands

The glorious islands of Scotland, stretching from the Clyde estuary and all the way up the west coast and beyond to Orkney and Shetland, boast some of the most beautiful nine-hole golf courses in the world. It is more difficult and expensive to get to the islands but the glorious scenery, the wildlife and the friendliness of the people, not to mention the beautiful courses, will all make it worthwhile. There are 23 courses in our list with four in the group that includes Barra, the Uists, and Benbecula, four on Orkney, three in Arran, two each on Bute, Mull and Skye and one each on the islands of Seil, Tiree, Coll, Harris and Shetland. Every one offers dramatic views and a demanding test, where mountains, seascapes, boats and vast horizons can all prove wonderfully distracting. Island courses are truly the nirvana of nine-hole golf.

Isle of Bute

This tour starts with the courses of Bute in the Clyde and works its way up the west coast to Shetland. Bute is reached by ferry from Wemyss Bay which takes 35 minutes. There is a shorter ferry crossing from Colintraive.

156 Port Bannatyne golf course was founded in 1912 and looks over Kames Bay to the Cowal Hills and the entrances of the Kyles of Bute and Loch Striven. At the top of the course there are views westward to Loch Fyne and the peninsula of Kintyre. This is an unusual layout with 13 holes, the first five being replayed before ending on a separate 18th. The holes are an interesting and demanding mix with many intriguing names, such as 'the Burn', 'the Rushes', 'the Kyles', 'the Pancake', 'the Winney', 'the Puzzle', 'the Trap' and 'the Saucer'. Located on the west coast and benefiting from the northern drift

156
Port Bannatyne

Est: 1912

Tel: **01700 504544**

Bannatyne Mains Road, Isle of Bute, PA20 0PH
Contact: **The Secretary**
Website: **www.portbannatynegolfclub.co.uk**
Terrain: **Inland**
Length m **4,506**
Par/SSS m **68/65**
Par 3 m **1**
Par 5 m **0**
Location: Two miles from Rothesay on A844

C B CHR P

C Clubhouse B Bar BG Buggy CH Club Hire T Trolley CHR Changing Rooms SHW Showers

Airthrey Golf Course

of the Gulf Stream the climate is temperate and the course is rarely closed for play.

Some six miles from Rothesay, the Island capital, is the Isle of Bute **157 Kingarth** course established in 1888. This is a flat links type course with pasture and gorse on several holes but little rough, and excellent greens. There is a small wooden clubhouse with changing facilities. The Captain's favourite and the signature hole is the third, a PAR 3 along the water's edge, across a burn, to the green and has views to the mountains of Arran. The course record is 62, six strokes below par, set in June 2000 by Graham Bolton the secretary/treasurer of Argyll and Bute Golf Union.

Isle of Arran

Arran is reached by ferry from Ardrossan to Brodick and takes about 55 minutes.

The **158 Corrie** golf course is at Sannox, on the A841 north from Brodick, the capital of the island. Founded in 1892 it is a short, hilly, wooded moorland course with heather rough and tight fairways. The course is in good condition and features high quality greens with hidden borrows. Views extend across the Firth of Clyde and into Argyll. The signature hole is the sixth, a 320 yard PAR 4 sloping sharply from left to right and slightly uphill. Watch out for the heather bordering the fairway while the prevailing wind can sometimes prove a problem. Red deer, hare and birds of prey can all be seen.

Across the far side of the island on 'The String' road which runs from Brodick is the **159 Shiskine** Golf and Tennis Club at Blackwaterfoot. This unspoiled links course set in magnificent scenery overlooking the Kilbrannan sound and the Mull of Kintyre is an unusual 12 hole layout. In recent years it has twice achieved the distinction of being ranked as one of the top 100 courses in Britain. In outstanding condition, the course measures 2,787 yards with a PAR of 42.

157 Kingarth

Est: 1888

Tel: **01700 502158**

St Ninians, 32 Marine Place, Ardbeg, Rothesay, Isle of Bute, PA20 0LF
Contact: **Fraser Robinson**
Email: **administrator@butegolfclub.com**
Website: **www.butegolfclub.com**
Terrain: **Links, with some gorse and pasture**
Length m **4,722**   Length l **4,510**
Par/SSS m **68/64**   Par/SSS l **68/69**
Rec m **62**
Par 3 m **2**   Par 3 l **2**
Par 5 m **0**   Par 5 l **0**

Signature Hole: Third, PAR 3 along waters edge, across burn to green. Views across Sound of Bute to the Mountains of Arran.

Captain's Hole: Third.

Times to Avoid: Before 11.30 on Saturdays

Clubhouse: Small, with changing facitities

Condition: Excellent greens, gorse bushes a problem.

Memorabilia: Yes, from Rothesay Golf Club

Wildlife: Seabirds, wild geese, swans, seals, hare, occasionaly deer.

Location: Six miles from Rothesay on A845 at Strathanan Bay, course signposted.

Accommodation: St Blane's Hotel, Kilchattan Bay, Kingarth Hotel, Kingarth.

Lost ball: 2

Comments: Splendid greens, wonderful views, a unique experience.

Clubs visiting: Contact Secretary

Caps visiting: Contact Secretary

C CHR

158 Corrie

Est: 1892

Tel: **01770 810606**

Corrie, Sannox, Isle of Arran, KA27 8JD
Contact: **G.E. Welford**
Email: **cmberrie@aol.com**
Website: **www.corriegolfclub.co.uk**
Terrain: **Moorland**
Length m **3,896**   Length l **3,275**
Par/SSS m **62/61**
Par 3 m **5**
Par 5 m **0**

Location: North of Brodick

C CHR CTR PG

159 Shiskine

Est: Unknown

Tel: **01770 860226**

Blackwaterfoot, Isle of Arran, KA27 8HA
Contact: **The Secretary**
Email: **info@shiskinegolf.com**
Website: **www.shishkinegolf.co.uk**
Terrain: **Links**
Length m **2,787** (12 holes)
Par/SSS m **42/42**
Par 3 m **3**
Par 5 m **0**

Location: On B880 11 miles from Brodick

C BG CH CHR CTR PG

Tobermory Golf Club
second green and third tee

Three miles north of Blackwaterfoot on the A841 is **160 Machrie Bay** golf course, a seaside links designed by William Fernie which stretches 4,556 yards with a PAR/SSS of 66/62. The amateur record is a wonderful 59, but this is overshadowed by the professional record of 53 held by Walter Hagen, the US Ryder Cup captain. The first hole 'Kilbrannan', a 319 yard PAR 4, has a road running along one side and the sea along the other and is described by the Captain as a 'very hard opening hole'. This is both the signature hole and the Captains favourite. There is a recently refurbished clubhouse which now has disabled changing rooms and provides refreshments and light meals but has no license.

The lush nine-holer at **161 Lochranza** to the north of Island is clearly a favourite hide-a-way for Scottish football stars. Murdo MacLeod the Celtic mid-fielder and Scottish international, and ex-Ranger Billy Dodds have both enjoyed this rugged course. The course was established by Lochranza villagers in 1898 and stretches along the even parkland of the glen towards the head of the sea loch. Its challenges include four fairways that cross the mountain burn. The course is in a National Scenic Area and Site of Importance for Nature Conservation.

Isle of Gigha

A Ferry runs from Tayinloan to the Isle of Gigha very regularly and takes 20 minutes.

Seven miles long by a mile and a half wide the island is three miles west of the Kintyre peninsular and is the most southerly of the Inner Hebridean islands. Following a successful buyout it is now a community owned island. The **162 Gigha** golf course was established in 1989 and has a parkland style with gently undulating fairways. 'The Road Hole' fourth, a 353 PAR 4 has out-of-bounds along the right of the fairway and a semi-blind but brave tee shot is rewarded. The Captain's choice is the PAR 4

160
Machrie Bay

Est: 1900

Tel: **01770 840329**

Machrie Bay, c/o The Estate Office, Dougarie, Isle of Arran, KA27 8EB
Contact: **S.C. Gibbs**
Email: **machriebayclubsec@googlemail.com**
Website: **www.machriebay.com**
Terrain: **Parkland**

Length m **4,556**	Length l **4,234**
Par/SSS m **66/62**	Par/SSS l **66/62**
Par 3 m 3	Par 3 l 3
Par 5 m 0	Par 5 l 0

Signature Hole: First, along the shore bounded by road on one side and the sea shore on the other.

Captain's Hole: First, difficult opening shot especially from competition tees.

Clubhouse: Newly renovated with good facilities. No bar.

Condition: Excellent

Memorabilia: Yes

Wildlife: Seals, porpoises, ducks, geese, swans and all common sea birds.

Location: Three miles north of Blackwaterfoot

Accommodation: Kinloch Hotel and Blackwaterfoot Lodge

Lost ball: 2/3

Comments: Very well maintained course in a beautiful setting

Discount: Arran Golf Pass

Clubs visiting: Contact Secretary

Caps visiting: Yes

C BG CH T CHR CTR PG P

C Clubhouse **B** Bar **BG** Buggy **CH** Club Hire **T** Trolley **CHR** Changing Rooms **SHW** Showers

161
Lochranza

Est: 1898

Tel: **01770 830 273**

Lochranza Golf Course, Lochranza, Isle of Arran, KA27 8HL

Contact: **Kathryn Mawson**

Email: **office@lochgolf.demon.co.uk**

Website: **www.lochranzagolf.com**

Terrain: **Parkland**

Length: **4,664 yards**

Par/SSS **68/68**

Catering: Stags Pavilion Restaurant adjacent to course.

Times to Avoid: Course closed from end October to Easter.

Wildlife: Lots! Red Deer, Golden Eagles, Red Squirrels

Location: Opposite Isle of Arran Distillery

Accommodation: Lochranza Hotel, Apple Lodge, Kincardine Lodge, Castlekirk and various B. and B's.

Secretary's Comments: Stunning scenery, lots of variety, challenge for all abilities, families welcome.

CTR T PG

162
Gigha

Est: 1989

Tel: **01583 505242**

The Golf Course, Isle of Gigha, Argyll, PA41 7AA

Contact: **John Bannatyne**

Email: **johngigha@hotmail.co.uk**

Website: **www.gigha.org**

Terrain: **Parkland, gently undulating fairways**

Length m **5,042**		Length l **4,620**
Par/SSS m **65/65**		Par/SSS l **66/66**
Rec m **70**		
Par 3 m **3**		Par 3 l **3**
Par 5 m **0**		Par 5 l **0**

Signature Hole: Fourth, out-of-bounds on right semi-blind but brave tee shot is rewarded

Captain's Hole: Seventh, panoramic views of Kintyre and Knaphill across the Sound of Gigha. Challenging PAR 4 with well guarded green.

Times to Avoid: Sunday 1 – 3pm

Clubhouse: Small

Condition: Summer good; spring and autumn fair

Wildlife: Birds of prey, hedgehogs, rabbits

Location: Close to ferry terminal, well signposted.

Accommodation: Isle of Gigha Hotel

Lost ball: 2

Comments: Visiting a beautiful island and enjoying a peaceful game on a well maintained course.

Fame: Neil Warnock, Manager, Sheffield United

Discount: Bunkered two for one

Clubs visiting: 25 per cent reduction for 12 or more

CH T CHR P

seventh 'Drumyeonbeg' which measures 310 yards with bunkers guarding the green. This hole has views of Kintyre and Knapdale and looks across the Sound of Gigha.

Isle of Seil

Travelling from Oban on the A816 to Kilninver, then the B8844 takes you to our next destination.

Although the **163 Isle of Seil** is joined to the mainland by the romantic 'Bridge over the Atlantic' we have given it the benefit of the doubt and included it in the island section of the guide. The 4,282 yard PAR 62 course is a challenging coastal layout, playing around Balvicar Bay and its slate quarries which opened for play in 1996. Several of the holes play across water and two of them over the sea, the eighth being a superb PAR 3. At least there are no bunkers and there is also the advantage of wonderful views, especially of the Isle of Mull. If your companions cannot face the rigours of nine-hole golf pack them off to Ellenabeich where they can chance their luck on the 12 Isles Putting Green – if they beat the PAR of 24 they could win a bottle of whisky! At the very least they will learn the names of the Scottish islands and they could even take the ferry across to the Easdale Island with its museum and tea room.

Isle of Mull

There are three car ferries serving the Isle of Mull. The main one runs from Oban to Craignure and takes 44 minutes. A smaller, cheaper and more frequent service departing from Lochaline to Fishnish, while to the north there is a ferry from Kilchoan to Tobermory, a journey of 35 minutes.

Situated on the site of an earlier course the new **164 Craignure** layout was re-designed in the late 1970's by David Howitt, a local hotelier and first captain of the new club and by Ian Phillips. Mrs Violet de Klee, whose family had laid out the original

163
Isle of Seil

Est: 1995

Tel: **01852 300348**

Balvicar, by Oban, PA34 4TL
Contact: **B. Mitchell/D. Nathan**
Terrain: **Coastal**

Length m **4,282**		Length I **1,944**
Par/SSS m **62/62**		Par/SSS I **62/62**
Par 3 m **5**		Par 3 I **5**
Par 5 m **0**		Par 5 I **0**

Signature Hole: Eighth, PAR 3 played from elevated tee, over inlet to green guarded by slate beach and small quarry

Captain's Hole: Fifth, PAR 4 dog-leg with a drive over water with out-of-bounds on right.

Clubhouse: Club Cabin with information

Condition: Improving, can be soft in winter

Memorabilia: Golf balls at Balvicar Stores

Location: Easily found on island

Accommodation: Stay at Willowburn Hotel, eat at Tigh-an-Truish Hotel

Lost ball: 3

Comments: Quiet course in a beautiful setting.

Clubs visiting: Contact Secretary

C CH

164
Craignure

Est: 1970's

Tel: **01680 812370**

Scallastle, Craignure, Isle of Mull, PA64 6AP
Contact: **The Secretary**
Email: **info@craignuregolfclub.co.uk**
Website: **www.craignuregolfclub.co.uk**
Terrain: **Links**
Length m **5,227**
Par/SSS m **67/66**
Par 3 m **3**
Par 5 m **1**
Location: One mile west of ferry terminal at Craignure

C B CH CHR P

Craignure Golf Course

Strathendrick Golf Course

course in 1895, hit the opening tee shot to a fly-past of small aircraft from the Island's airstrip. A dramatic picture in the clubhouse shows Mrs de Klee at the completion of her strike with the ball leaving the tee and framed by the approaching aircraft above. The course is situated just a few miles north of the Craignure ferry terminal to the seaward side of the main Tobermory road and follows the natural sweep of the bay. It is parkland with links characteristics and some very demanding holes. As usual with links courses the weather has a quite disproportionate effect on the difficulties. The sixth and seventh holes are most typical of the nature of this fine layout both demanding accurate shots from the tee and tricky carries over the lurking hazards.

If man and nature ever conspired to create the perfect golf course it must have been at **165 Tobermory**. You have to indulge me here for this is my home course and one which my wife and I have played for over 30 years. On the hill above the town, famous for its colourful houses, fishing boats and TV programme Balamory, the course is a mixture of hill and heath and described in the Herald newspaper as a 'course with a view that beats par'. From various tees the view captures Tobermory Bay, the Sound of Mull, Morvern, Ardnamurchan and even, on the surprisingly frequent fine days, the mountains of the cocktail islands of Rhum and Eigg.

Approach the signature seventh with care; it is a hole with sharp teeth, always ready to bite. A short PAR 3, it demands a pin-point tee shot to the small green on the far side of the gulley with out-of-bounds to the right and a rocky outcrop to the rear. A PAR 3 here sends a curly whirly thrill up the spine. The first is one of the trickiest openers anywhere, with a tee shot climbing two banks to a broad fairway, and then a second across a gulley to the green. But it is the second, the Captain's choice, which challenges even the best golfer. A long tee shot across another gulley to a broad fairway, and then a demanding second to

165
Tobermory

Est: 1896

Tel: **01688 302741**

Erray Road, Tobermory, Isle of Mull, PA75 6PS
Contact: **Gordon Chalmers**
Email: **secretary@tobermorygolfclub.com**
Website: **www.tobermorygolfclub.com**
Terrain: **Heath and heather, rugged**

Length m **4,912**		Length l **4,344**
Par/SSS m **64/64**		Par/SSS l **68/66**
Rec m **65**		
Par 3 m **4**		Par 3 l **3**
Par 5 m **0**		Par 5 l **1**

Signature Hole: Seventh, tricky PAR 3 across gully, out-of-bounds on right, rock face at rear of green

Times to Avoid: Saturday/Sunday afternoons in summer

Clubhouse: Good facilities, open dawn to dusk, visitors changing room, toilet, limited catering in summer

Condition: Excellent, full time green keeper

Memorabilia: Ball markers, pitch repairers, polo shirts

Wildlife: Buzzards, golden eagles, numerous small birds, orchids

Location: Top of the town on Erray Rd., well signposted

Accommodation: Numerous good accommodation and restaurants in town

Lost ball: 3

Comments: Unspoilt, beautifully maintained, virtually no restrictions and unrivalled views

Fame: Tom Watson, Bill MacLaren

C CH CHR CTR PG P

C Clubhouse B Bar BG Buggy CH Club Hire T Trolley CHR Changing Rooms SHW Showers

Tobermory Golf Course
second and third greens

a small green tucked behind rocks and rough, with the ground sloping away at the front. Altogether a course to be enjoyed at leisure.

Tiree

The ferry from Oban takes four hours to reach Tiree.

Sitting further west in the Atlantic than Mull is the island of Tiree and as the traditional song would have it:

'The boat leaves Oban every day
Passing Tobermory on the way
Onwards to the lovely Isle of Coll
To Tiree, the most beautiful of all'

Tiree is famous these days as one of the windsurfing capitals of Europe, which gives some idea of the wind blowing constantly over this low-lying sandy oasis. The lovely little **166 Vaul** golf course at Scarinish was originally laid out by the navy in 1886. It is a reasonably flat course on the machair, which is a distinctive type of coastal grassland found in the north and west of Scotland. In the springtime it comes alive with wild flowers scattered liberally over the fairways which can make it difficult to find your ball even when played straight down the middle. There are no trees or water hazards, just a leisurely round of golf with the anticipation of refreshment in the local hotel. Watch out for

166
Vaul

Est: 1886

Tel: **01879 220729**

Scarinish, Isle of Tiree, Argyll, PA77 6XH
Contact: **The Secretary**
Email: **kirkapoltiree@aol.com**
Website: **www.vaulgolfclub.org**
Terrain: **Links**

Length m **5,788**	Length l **5,152**
Par/SSS m **72/68**	Par/SSS l **72/71**
Par 3 m 1	Par 3 l 1
Par 5 m 1	Par 5 l 1

Location: Two miles from Scaranish, half a mile from Lodge Hotel

C CHR PG P

Craignure Golf Course

C Clubhouse B Bar BG Buggy CH Club Hire T Trolley CHR Changing Rooms SHW Showers

Vaul Golf Course fourth tee

corncrakes, one of Britain's rarest birds, which find a home here.

Skye

There are several ways to get to Skye, the Skye Bridge (no longer with a toll to pay), the ferry from Mallaig to Armadale takes about 25 minutes, a six car ferry from Glenelg to Kylerhea runs regularly from April to October and a ferry runs from Uig to Tarbert, Harris.

The Isle of Skye golf course near **167 Sconser** at the centre of the island on the A87, is a seaside links course with extensive views of the Red Cuillin hills and across the Sound of Raasay. A feature of this fine course is that several holes have alternative tee positions second time around, giving a different approach and length, and the feel of an 18 hole course. The signature hole is the 349 yard PAR 4 sixth with a 100 yard carry over a stream and another to navigate 100 yards further on. The second shot is to a bunkered green. The second, the Captain's favourite, is another PAR 4 which often lays into the wind and has out-of-bounds to the left of the fairway.

There is a basic clubhouse with visitor changing room, small shop and café. Plenty of wildlife here too, with ducks, wading birds, seals and occasionally dolphins to brighten the day.

Situated in the grounds of the Skeabost House Hotel close to Portree on the A850 the parkland **168 Skeabost** course is constructed on a site where a fierce battle was once fought between the MacDonalds and the MacLeods. Things are more peaceful now on this short course where the only battle is likely to be between yourself and your swing. There are a few bunkers to catch the unwary shot but few other hazards. The pick of the holes is the very short fourth, the 'Glory Hole' which is just 91 yards long, played to a green guarded by both bunkers and trees.

167
Sconser

Est: 1964

Tel: **01478 650414**

Sconser, Isle of Skye, IV48 8TD
Contact: **Ian Marr**
Email: **info@isleofskyegolfclub.co.uk**
Website: **www.isleofskyegolfclub.co.uk**
Terrain: **Seaside**

Length m **4,677**	Length l **4,313**
Par/SSS m **66/64**	Par/SSS l **66/65**
Rec m **63**	
Par 3 m **6**	Par 3 l **6**
Par 5 m **0**	Par 5 l **0**

Signature Hole: Sixth, 349 yard PAR 4 with 100 yard carry over a stream and another 100 yards further on. Second shot to a bunkered green, with trees on the left and o.o.b. all the way on the right.

Captain's Hole: Second, 447 yard PAR 4 often lays into the wind, dog-leg left, o.o.b. all the way on the left. PAR 4's are very rare.

Times to Avoid: Tuesday afternoons, Wednesday evenings, Saturday and Sunday 9.45

Clubhouse: Basic, with visitor changing rooms, small shop and café.

Condition: Very good in summer, can be wet after a rainy spell.

Memorabilia: Yes

Wildlife: Ducks, wading birds, seals and occasionally dolphins.

Location: On main A87 near Sconser.

Accommodation: Check with Tourist Info.

Lost ball: 2

Comments: Beautiful views to Red Cuillin hills and over Sound of Raasay

Clubs visiting: Contact Secretary

Caps visiting: Contact Secretary

C CH T CHR SHW CTR PG P

168
Skeabost

Est: Unknown

Tel: **01470 532202**

Skeabost House Hotel, Skeabost Bridge, Isle of
Skye, IV51 9NP
Contact: **The Secretary**
Email: **manager.skeabost@ohiml.com**
Website: **www.oxfordhotelsandinns.com**
Terrain: **Wooded parkland**
Length m **3,224**
Par/SSS m **62/59**
Par 3 m **5**
Par 5 m **0**
Location: Off the A850 Portree to Dunvegan
  road

B CH T CTR

Craignure Golf Course

Barra, Uist and Benbecula

The ferry from Oban to Castlebay takes 5 hours 20 minutes and from Barra to Uist takes 1 hour 50 minutes. There is a scheduled air service from Glasgow and the islands are linked by causeways.

The **169 Barra** golf course, established in 1992, is situated at Cleat on the west coast of the island, six miles from Castlebay and close to the Isle of Barra Hotel. It is the most westerly course in the United Kingdom. Built on the machair the natural turf provides an excellent playing surface for the 4,792 yard course with a PAR/SSS of 68/64. At the moment there is no clubhouse but one is planned as part of a millennium project. The course enjoys views across the beach and out into the Atlantic.

To the north the next course is **170 Askernish** on the west coast of South Uist adjacent to 20 miles of silver shell beach. This is another course originally laid out by Old Tom Morris who described it as 'second to none in the various elements which go to make up a really good course'. There is some doubt as to whether this course should be included in this guide as there are actually two nine-hole courses and the score card treats them as a single 18 hole course. Still, we will give it the benefit of the doubt as visitors can make their own choice as to how many holes they play. The Bunker House

169
Barra

Est: 1992

Tel: **01871 810419**

Cleat Castle, Isle of Barra, HS9 5XX
Contact: **The Secretary**
Email: **duncanmackinnon@live.co.uk**
Website: **www.isleofbarra.com/golf1**
Terrain: **Links**
Length m **4,792**
Par/SSS m **68/64**
Location: Six miles from Castlebay

CH T

Balgove Course, St Andrews

170
Askernish

Est: Unknown

Tel: **01878 700083**

Lochboisdale, Askernish, South Uist, HS81 5ST
Contact: **The Secretary**
Email: **info@askernishgolfclub.com**
Website: **www.askernishgolfclub.com**
Terrain: **Links**
Length m **6,167**
Par/SSS m **72/67**
Par 3 m **3**
Par 5 m **0**
Location: Five miles north west of Lochboisdale

C CH T CHR PG

Bridge of Allan Golf Club

situated by the gate at the entrance offers changing facilities but no toilet.

North-west from here and between the South and North Uists is **171 Benbecula** which has been dominated by the military for years, and it is work provided at the airport which accounts for the relatively high population on the island. For many years the M.O.D. was responsible for the maintenance of the course and while it may not now have the short-back-and-sides of earlier days it is still well tended. The course is situated by the air strip and close to the main town of Balivanich. On flat ground, the course makes for an easy, relaxed round of golf with few hazards.

Since the *Nine-Holer Guide* was first published the delightful **172 Sollas** course situated on the north west coast of North Uist overlooking the Atlantic, has been reclaimed as farming land. The course was built and maintained by local volunteers in the summer of 2001 on the machair used by local crofters who gave permission for the lovely little layout. Now it has been partially ploughed over and none of the holes are playable. Very sad, but there are local people who still believe that one day they will be able to swing a club on their own course once again. Fingers crossed!

Harris

The ferry from Uig, Skye, to Tarbert on Harris runs daily and takes 1 hour 40 minutes. You can also travel by road from Lewis.

173 Scarista Golf Course on the Isle of Harris is the most northerly nine-hole course on the west coast of Scotland and enjoys a breathtaking situation on the west coast of the island. There are views of spectacular mountains and the thunder of Atlantic breakers offers a noisy background to your game. A links course, set on the machair behind the beach, this demanding layout has attracted many famous names and has been compared to Augusta National and the Old Course at St Andrews. Nick Faldo played

171
Benbecula

Est: Unknown

Tel: **01870 603275**

Balivanich, Benbecula, HS7 5LA
Contact: **The Secretary**
Email: **enquiries@benbeculagolfclub.co.uk**
Website: **www.benbeculagolfclub.co.uk**
Terrain: **Links**
Length m **4,380**
Par/SSS m **62/63**

Location: One mile north of Benbecula Airport

C CH P

172
Sollas

Est: 2001

Sollas, North Uist, Outer Hebrides
Contact: **The Secretary**
Terrain: **Machair**
Length m **3,888**　　　　Length l **3,888**
Par/SSS m **66/66**　　　Par/SSS l **66/66**
Par 3 m **3**　　　　　　Par 3 l **3**
Par 5 m **0**　　　　　　Par 5 l **0**

Times to Avoid: Very few

Condition: Cows and sheep graze the machiar in the winter!

Location: Easily found

CH

173
Scarista

Est: 1987

Tel: **01859 550226**

Scarista, Isle of Harris, Western Isles, HS3 3HT
Contact: **John MacLean**
Email: **harrisgolf@ic24.net**
Website: **www.harrisgolf.com**
Terrain: **Links/machair**
Length m **4,904**　　　　Length l **4,188**
Par/SSS m **68/64**　　　Par/SSS l **68/62**
Rec m **61**　　　　　　Rec l **85**
Par 3 m **3**　　　　　　Par 3 l **3**
Par 5 m **1**　　　　　　Par 5 l **1**

Times to Avoid: Very few

Clubhouse: WC and primus stove

Condition: Continually being improved

Memorabilia: Yes

Wildlife: Seals, otters, buzzards, eagles and sea birds

Location: On west coast of island

Accommodation: Good choice

Lost ball: 3

Comments: Good scenery and wildlife – old fashioned links course

Fame: Nick Faldo, Rohann Rafferty

C CH T CHR

Vaul Golf Course

here in the early 90s and his green fee 'The Faldo Fiver' is the trophy for an annual competition at the club, while more recently Ronan Rafferty played the course and his golf ball has also been turned into a trophy. It goes without saying that the golf is hugely enjoyable and there is the chance of spotting seals, otters, buzzards, eagles and a wealth of other wildlife. The rough is fierce in this remote spot, while the clubhouse is a renovated shipping container. The course is 15 miles south of the ferry at Tarbert and is worth every minute of the drive.

Orkney

Ferries run twice daily in the summer from Aberdeen to Kirkwall and from Kirkwall to Sanday and Westray. There are also air services daily from Aberdeen and Inverness. The journey to South Ronaldsay is overland whist there is a weekly ferry to North Ronaldsay.

There are four nine-holers in the Orkney islands. South Ronaldsay is on the southern-most island, connected by road to the main island, and then moving north Sanday is to the north-west, Westray to the north-east and North Ronaldsay is about as far north as it is possible to go in the Orkneys. The last three courses require ferries from Kirkwall although some flights are available.

After seven years hard work the **174 South Ronaldsay** course, in the village of St Margaret's Hope, was opened in June 2005 when the first ball was struck by Club Captain Jim Seatter and more than 100 players enjoyed the inaugural competition with support from members of the Orkney and Stromness Golf Clubs. The parkland course measures 5,508 yards with a PAR/SSS of 66/67 and is situated at Neviholm, Hoxa. The third is one of the most difficult holes on the course with the wind, burns and ditches adding to the difficulties.

One mile north of Pierowall off the B9066 is the enjoyable seaside links course of **175 Westray**.

174
South Ronaldsay

Est: 2005
Tel: **01856 831395**
Neviholm, Hoxa, South Ronaldsay, Orkney, KW17 2TW
Contact: **The Secretary**
Terrain: **Parkland**
Length m **5,508**
Par/SSS m **66/67**
Par 3 m **3**
Par 5 m **0**
Location: In village of St Margaret's Hope

C CH T CHR CTR PG P

C Clubhouse B Bar BG Buggy CH Club Hire T Trolley CHR Changing Rooms SHW Showers

Est: Unknown

Tel: **01857 677373**

Westray, Orkney, KW17 2DH
Contact: **The Secretary** Billy Tulloch
Terrain: **Links**
Length m **4,810**
Par/SSS m **66/66**
Location: One mile north-west of Pierowall of B9066

C CH

Golfer being attacked at
Sanday Golf Course

Relatively flat, this is an easy walking course where the main hazards are the rabbit holes. When we last checked the green fees were less than a fiver a day, so golf does not come much cheaper than this. The course measures 4,810 yards and with a PAR/SSS of 66.

Two miles north of Lady on the B9069 is **176 Sanday** Golf Club which claims to be the smallest in Scotland. With just six to eight regular playing members who are we to argue? Roderick Thorne, the enthusiastic secretary, tells us that the Club's logo is the Arctic Skua, a pair of which nest every year on the line of the parallel first and second holes. 'This is a pretty aggressive species when eggs have been laid or are hatched. In May and June players usually hold a short-iron aloft in order to avoid having the scalp whacked by a skua's feet!' This must be one of the more unusual hazards on a golf course. In summer the ground is an array of links flowers and in addition to the Skua a variety of other birds breed on the course, including ringed plover, oystercatcher, fulmar, common gull, black-headed gull, arctic tern and occasionally even eider duck. The signature hole is the first, 'Big John', named after John Stark, the golf pro at Crieff who visited several times to advise on the links layout.

Having spoken to the tourist information office in Kirkwall it is clear that there is a nine-holer in **177 North Ronaldsay**, but so far I have been unable to find out much about it. It appears to be a links course measuring 4,424 yards and has a PAR/SSS of 70. And a day ticket costs only £3. To find it go north from the pier and then a sharp right at the war memorial. After the post office go to the end of the world. Oops! that should read, end of the road.

Shetland

To reach Shetland there are ferries daily from Aberdeen to Lerwick.

Established in 1992 **178 Asta** golf course is a

176
Sanday

Est: 1977

Tel: **01857 600341**

Nearhouse, Sanday, Orkney, KW17 2BW
Contact: **Roderick Thorne**
Email: **orkneygolfclub@yahoo.com**
Website: **www.orkneygolfclub.co.uk**
Terrain: **Links**
Length m **5,200**   Length l **5,200**
Par/SSS m **70/72**
Rec m **34** (9 holes)
Par 3 m **3**
Par 5 m **2**

Signature Hole: First, 'Big John', named after John Stark the Crieff professional who advised on course layout and with childrens tuition.

Captain's Hole: Seventh, 'Chalois' named after the oystercatcher and where the tee shot on this PAR 3 can vary from an eight iron to a three wool!

Clubhouse: Limited facilities

Condition: No fairways, but reasonable greens. Course shared sometimes with cattle and sheep and always the birds.

Wildlife: Plentiful birdlife including Artic Skuas, and varied plant life including orchids.

Location: Easy to find.

Accommodation: 23 good hotels, hostel, quality self-catering and B and B's.

Lost ball: 10

Comments: Fantastic wildlife, annual membership £10 and no further green fees.

C P

177
North Ronaldsay

Est: Unknown

Tel: **01857 633242**

North Ronaldsay, Orkney,
Contact: **P. Donnelly**
Terrain: **Links**
Length m **4,424**
Par/SSS m **70/70**

178
Asta

Est: 1992

Tel: **01595 880231**

Garth Burn, Asta, Scalloway, Shetland,
Contact: **Jim Leask**
Email: **astagolfclub@btinternet.com**
Terrain: **Flat, easy walking**

Length m **4,058**	Length l **3,478**
Par/SSS m **62/62**	
Par 3m **6**	Par 3l **6**
Par 5m **1**	Par 5l **1**

Clubhouse: Small clubhouse with toilets

Condition: Good in summer

Wildlife: Birdlife

Location: Two miles north of Scalloway village

Accommodation: Herrislea House, Tingwall or
Scalloway Hotel

Comments: Very scenic, easy walking beside
two lochs.

Clubs visiting: Contact Secretary

C B CH CTR P

Oystercatcher chic

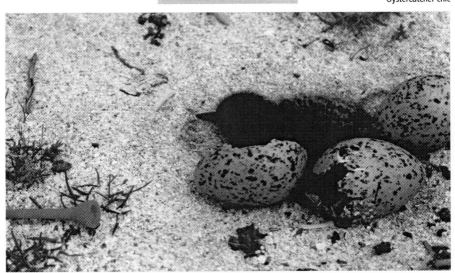

scenic, easy walking parkland course beside two lochs, Asta and Dingwall. Situated one mile north of the village Scalloway it is well-maintained during the summer and measures 4,056 yards with a PAR/SSS of 62/62. There is a small clubhouse with limited facilities and the course enjoys easy access, good parking facilities and is in a quiet peaceful area. There is abundant wildlife here, particularly many species of birds; ducks, geese and swans. Wind is always a feature on this lovely little course and the views and the welcome ensure a happy day out.

Clubhouse Seil Island

Tarbat Club House

INDEX

Pilgrims in the Rough: An Unreliable History of St Andrews

Michael Tobert
ISBN 978 1 906817 96 1
PBK £7.99

Pilgrims: people in search of the truth, a truth, any truth.

Rough: where not-so-good golfers find themselves from time to time

History: sometimes reliable, sometimes not, always subjective.

St Andrews: a charming and historic town on the east coast of Scotland; site of the Chariots of Fire beach; the home of golf; as close to paradise as you're likely to find this side of the pearly gates.

Q. Why should I buy this book?

A. You'll love it.

MICHAEL TOBERT

While *Pilgrims in the Rough* is more than just a guide to clubs and caddies, it is nonetheless packed with information for the golf enthusiast. It features a detailed map of the course and the low down from a regular St Andrews player on booking times, the clubs and each of the holes on the notorious Old Course. The book also contains an informative guide to the attractions of the town and the best places to stay and to eat out. Michael Tobert's infectious enthusiasm for St Andrews will even persuade the most jaded golf widow or widower that the town is worth a visit!

The Mating-Call of the Racket Tailed Drongo

Michael Tobert
ISBN 978 1906307 50 9
PBK £8.99

Mating Call: a device for attracting the female.

Racket-Tailed Drongo: a devious bird – not always what it seems.

Featuring:
Janet (and her virginity)
The August and Venerable Golf Club of St Magnus
Archie (the official seducer)
Alistair (the Secretary that spills the beans)
Not to mention, the Kama Sutra, fish, snakes tsunamis, Sanskrit
And of course Pottle (and all his woes)

The August and Venerable Golf Club of St Magnus is in trouble. In an ancient deed the Secretary discovers that the clubhouse and land will revert back to Janet, the fishmonger's daughter, if, on her 18th birthday, she is still a virgin. The birthday is imminent, and the Secretary decides to take matters into his own hands…

A wry, hilarious comedy of manners, with more coils than an Indian python.

… funny, clever, learned, human and surprising take on the genre. Which one? The nonsense one, the one that probably began with Tristam Shandy, whose special blend of splashy understatement comes to mind easily when reading The Mating Call.
ST ANDREWS IN TOUCH

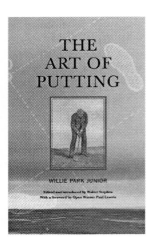

The Art of Putting

Willie Park Junior
(edited and introduced
by Walter Stephen)
ISBN 978 1905222 66 7
PBK £5.99

'The man who can putt is a match for anyone.' So said Willie Park in 1920, and it is still true today.

Willie Park's transcendent manual seeks to share the methods which made him 'the best and most consistent putter in the world'. Equipment may have changed and competition may be fiercer, but with Park's guidance, you too will have a fighting chance of making that all-important putt.

This guide to putting for players of all skill levels is fully illustrated; covers every aspect of putting, from grip to the lie of the green; and is a clear, concise and detailed guide to mastery of technique.

The Game of Golf

Willie Park Junior
(edited and introduced
by Walter Stephen)
ISBN 978 1905222 65 0
HBK £12.99

The golfer Willie Park Junior speaks out and voices his opinions on golfing equipment and techniques. Straight from the man who brought golf from Scotland to the world comes a comprehensive guide to playing golf that compliments the game of players of all skill levels.

Every aspect of playing, from selecting equipment to proper swing and grip, is explained in detail and given beside the opinion and tips of a successful 19th century golf champion. This commentary reveals the finer details of the game and original techniques that can still be applied today. Including a helpful glossary and diagrams and illustrations, the history and art of golf are revealed.